In a Perfect World

A Survival Guide for the Help Desk Technician

By D. Russell Steffy

NOTICE

Information in this document is subject to change without notice. Companies, names, and data used in examples herein are fictitious unless otherwise noted. No part of this document may be reproduced or transmitted in any form or by any means, electronic or mechanical, for any purpose, without the express written permission of **THE AUTHOR**. **THE AUTHOR** makes no warranty of any kind with regard to this material, including, but not limited to, the implied warranties of merchantability and fitness for a particular purpose. **THE AUTHOR** shall not be liable for errors contained herein or for incidental or consequential damages in connection with the furnishing, performance, or use of this material.

i

About this Guide

The scope of this guide focuses primarily towards offering those of all skill levels, who serve as the front line for corporate technical support, and with a light-hearted approach to common sense problem solving. The Help Desk is often the first impression a prospective client will experience, and it is imperative that all problems be resolved with expedience and professionalism, rather than rubber bands and paper clips.

This guide assumes the role of the IT Help Desk Technician to be one of perhaps four levels: Level I – novice, right out of school with no real world experience but is proficient with use of phones and email, Level II possesses a couple of years of experience and has memorized the company's universal troubleshooting checklist (assuming one exists), Level III understands basic concepts of common sense beyond the checklist, and Level IV doesn't give credibility to any checklists but *applies* advanced concepts of common sense, and likely has reached a plateau where the next step is perhaps a valuable role in management. This guide also assumes three basic environments: 1) the Help Desk Tech is exclusively for support of in-house personnel, 2) solely for support of a corporate product line, and 3) both in-house and outside users. I touch base on issues which bound the scope but are still related to technical issues. I include some pointers on the use of the computer at home with children, and I discuss the effort necessary to self publish this guide. I use real life experiences wherever possible for your entertainment and to provide you a clue with what you can expect in the not-so-perfect-world of the Help Desk Technician. So, fasten your seatbelts, here's a sample of what's in store for you:

Yup, this one's true. How could I possibly make this up? Besides, as you will see, I don't need to make anything up. There's no shortage of lack of common sense in the general populous. Anyway, the CEO buys a brand new 22 inch flat screen for himself and shows it off to everybody. I must admit, it was nice. Would've been nicer if he'd bought me one too. A couple of days later he calls me into his office and starts complaining about the "dead" pixels on his new monitor. He starts telling me to pack it up for him so he could return it. But, hold on! I take a closer look and discover that the dead pixels are just some splotches of soda. A little warm water on a cleaning wipe and I raised those pixels from the dead!

Shortly after I began employment as an assistant network administrator at a small distribution company, the Senior Vice President called me exclaiming "The browser keeps launching, over and over again! I keep closing the windows but it keeps launching! I can't keep up with it! Get over to my office now!" . Upon arriving at his office and confirming the reported problem, it took me about 10 seconds to notice that his keyboard, situated in a tray attached to the underside of his desk, was pinned such that the function key that launches the browser was in the depressed position. But, I am thankful for all the wing nuts, idiots, and morons, for they maintain job security for you and me.

Note: Names within this guide have been changed to protect the innocent, naïve, and technically challenged.

"It is better to remain silent and thought to be a fool than to speak and remove all doubt"
- Socrates

"Failure is merely success turned upside-down"
- Author Unknown

Forward

So, you wanted to become a highly paid Information Technology professional? Welcome to my world -- except for the "highly paid" part.

IT in general, and Technical Support in particular, are widely regarded by executive management as a necessary evil because it's overhead and doesn't generate any revenue. These are jobs where "no news is good news" usually applies. If you're looking for that occasional "pat on the back", consider another profession. Every time the phone rings or an email is received, it isn't because someone wants to pin a medal on your chest. Prepare for all of the handy work that doesn't work, the users who are going to whine at you because it doesn't work, the technical staff that has to fix their creations that don't work, and the boss who has to sign the paychecks for all who have to make things work. The challenge is to leave it all at the office when you go home for the day, or night.

It's not all discouraging. Resolving user's problems is rewarding. Remember, they're at the dirt-hit-the-fan end of the stick even before they call you. So you're a hero when you do get them back up and running.

When I started out in what is now commonly known as Information Technology, the field was generally referred to as "Information Processing". There were virtually no degrees offered in Computer Science, you had to pursue an Electrical Engineering degree to gain academic exposure to learning programming languages, operating system basics, and computer operations in general. I began my career while I was still in high school. I landed my first job as an assistant to the office staff through a bit of nepotism. I started out making copies of documents, taking out the trash, and running errands.

My big break was when their RJE operator quit showing up for work and I was asked if I was interested in the position, my decision was a big no-brainer. I had access to one of the most powerful mainframes at the time, a CDC 7600, as well as the latest mini-computer – a Data General SPC-16 with a whopping 32kb of memory and a 2mg hard drive (removable platter). The hard drive alone was about $20,000 in 1972 dollars.

In those days, the "sysgen" on a mini-computer was all important. You had to build the operating system from paper tape "bootstraps" followed by thousands of punch cards arranged in decks, like decks of playing cards, each loaded at a specific step in the process. You had to allocate so much memory for each peripheral, the card reader, the paper tape reader, printer, etc. The trick was not to exceed allocating more than 16kb of memory for all of the peripherals (more commonly known now as drivers), that's all you were allowed because the remaining 16kb was for running the actual software application. Very much like trying to stuff ten pounds of dirt in a five pound bag.

If the sysgen was successful, then you could punch a series of paper tapes (actually Mylar which was much more durable) for rebooting the next time without having to go through the whole sysgen process again. Instead of eight hours, it would take perhaps four. (Think about this the next time someone whines about their workstation taking five minutes to boot).

Thank the computer almighty for the introduction of the PC in the early 1980's. My first experience was a dual floppy, 8088 processor, no hard drive, running DOS version 1.0. At least it didn't take half a day to boot, and you had 512kb of memory – a considerable leap at the time.

One drawback with this machine was that if you left a non-bootable floppy in overnight, it would continue to attempt to reboot until the floppy shredded. Of course the rest is more recent history. IT Help Desk Technicians began to evolve significantly with the introduction of the Windows operating system and more stable networks in the mid 1990's.

Why am I touching a bit on history? I believe that understanding history assists with the basic understanding of how things work today. Like knowing how to do long division on paper so that you are not totally dependent on a calculator. Another example is: do you know how machine speeds achieved exponential increases in performance? Aside from just better electronics, how about the fact that components are constantly being packaged in smaller proximity? The speed of electricity (same as the speed of light) is finite. If you half the distance between the CPU and the hard drive, you have cut in half the amount of time it takes for a signal to travel between the two thus increasing performance. While we are capable of packaging components at ever decreasing sizes, what is one of the major problems encountered? Not so simple, how do you solve the problem of heat transfer? Many mainframes back in the 70's and 80's actually had a system of pipes carrying water to cool the electronics much like a radiator in a car. One mainframe was designed to be completely submerged in coolant. Another example of speed up is hard drive heads "fly" at a distance less than the width of a smoke particle from the platter. The closer the heads are to the platters, the faster the data is read and written. Hard drives resemble old record players, where the record is like one of the hard disk platters and the arm is like the drive head.

Table of Contents

Chapter 1 Defining Help Desk, Technical Support

I present in this chapter some basic strategies I believe will improve the overall effectiveness of the Help Desk department. I present a few definitions, a few tricks of the trade, tools, and hopefully a couple things that may even be entertaining.

Shortly after I began employment as an assistant network administrator at a small distribution company, the Senior Vice President yelled at me to get over to his office and fix his laptop. He continued yelling at me about how his laptop kept dying after about 20 minutes or so. He had tried three or four times to enter his data into a spreadsheet, only to lose it when it died. I waited for him to finish the tantrum he was throwing in front of the whole front office before pointing out that his laptop was unplugged (in front of the whole front office). The wing nut didn't understand that if you don't take proper care of the battery, or at least replace it, it's not going to last very long. And it's not going to work when unplugged. In his case, each of the times the laptop died, there was just enough charge to re-boot and enter about 20 minutes worth of work before it would shut down again. He didn't say a word as I left.

Common Sense

My good friend Steve posed an interesting question to me that he was asked in an interview: "In two sentences, or less, give me the definition of common sense." My nearly instantaneous reply was "never look up with you mouth open". Of course, this is really an analogy, not a definition.

I haven't yet found a definition of common sense. What I have found, is that a very large percentile of the population has very little of it. I bring this up because most of what Help Desk and Customer Support consists of is simply common sense.

Here are a couple more definitions of common sense by analogy:

Never kick a fresh pile of poop.
Never pee into the wind, but sometimes you just can't help it.
If your wife doesn't know what Dodger Dogs are, never let her prepare them.
When troubleshooting, never trust a spreadsheet from anyone.

As a network administrator in one small company, I wore many hats. I was responsible for everything that plugged into 110vac, RJ11C, RJ45, and a host of others. One morning while PM'ing our printers, I noticed a rather large, full cup of coffee sitting on top of one of MY $15,000 color copier/printers. I yelled across the room for the owner of the cup of coffee. Ernie fessed up, and I let him have it. "Ernie, do you have any idea what would happen if that cup of coffee were to spill into MY printer? First, we wouldn't have a printer, second, I would have to clean it up and attempt to get it working again. Third, if I can't get it working again, you're going to have to explain the $2,500.00 repair bill to the CEO". Never ceases to amaze me the lack of common sense in a lot of individuals.

Just a quick interesting note, one time I once had a tech on site to service one of these printer/copiers. He told me the most common call he gets around the holiday season was for the busted glass plate on top. The cause – folks trying to make a copy of their bare butt.

Skill Level

Level I techs should just start learning technique.
Level II techs start learning psychology.
Level III techs are skilled in levels I and II, but add policing and babysitting skills along with the ability to act with diplomacy.
Level IV techs are skilled in Level III, and have mastered common sense.

Client, Customer, User

Throughout this guide, I define "Client" as a way of referring more to an organization's executive management. "Customer" is a general reference to a middle manager, and a User is someone who is on the front lines, not in management.

Help Desk vs. Customer Service

I am not aware of any industry standard definitions of what a Help Desk Technicians' duties are versus a Customer Service Representative. As a Help Desk Tech, you are providing service to the customer, same as the Customer Service Rep. A similar level of professionalism should be provided by both departments. Those are the similarities. The difference is the Help Desk Tech will generally be committed entirely to resolving technical issues while the Customer Support Rep might be exclusively responsible for administrative issues such as entering orders and resolving accounting issues with the customer.

Chapter 2 Strategies for Support

Assuming the product(s) you support are mission critical for your users, be aware, no matter what the problem is – you are going to get the call.

Above and Beyond the Call

Occasionally, and depending on the circumstances, I might offer a freebee to an upset customer to keep him happy. I am not talking about giving away the entire product line, or spending weeks on some development project for free. I might give the latest version of the zip code database at no charge. Or perhaps a minor module, something with a low price point. I might spend an hour showing him user how to export data from the product I support, import that data into a spreadsheet, and build a few formulas to arrive at the desired results. The company's not going to go broke, and it makes for another happy customer.

Anti-Virus, Software Firewalls

I mention later on in this guide about an incident where I completely removed the anti-virus app altogether to resolve a problem. This is an extreme approach, normally all you need to do is disable the app long enough to test your app for conflicts with the antivirus app. Given that most error messages are cryptic at best, and worse may be misleading, it never hurts to perform this test early on in the troubleshooting stage. I also disable all software firewalls as well although I tend to not to make too many changes at once, otherwise I may not know for sure which change actually resolved the problem.

Although completely disabling firewalls and anti-virus apps is an extreme measure, I am only advocating this step as temporary – long enough to determine if this resolves the issue immediately. Other situations may dictate limiting what the firewall or antivirus app might affect. Adding specific applications or data folders to an exclusion list to test for a longer duration may be more appropriate. Opportunities to find exact cause are few and far between. I encourage taking advantage whenever possible, and always document the results.

Documentation

I describe later on about the importance of spelling, grammar, and punctuation in documentation. Here, I would like to offer my opinion on documentation from the perspective of the Help Desk Tech and the User.

Let's face it, nobody reads documentation. At least not in detail cover to cover, unless it's your job as a technical writer or some other related capacity. I emphasize that user's manuals and technical guides are primarily for reference. Hard copy documentation is obsolete, it's simply easier to use the Find function and specify a keyword to quickly arrive at the answer to a question. The only purpose I have for hard copy is to quickly and easily hand write notes regarding additions and changes to the document. And, hard copy in a notebook lets me visualize what the customer is going to receive in the event hard copy manuals are delivered with the application.

You can have the greatest user's guide ever known to man. But the vast majority of your users are not going to take advantage unless you apply a little constant pressure.

I accomplish this as often as possible by responding to inquires, that I know are well documented, with a reference to the exact chapter and page (or perhaps a link to a Knowledge Base article or FAQ on the company web site). I let them know that the User's Guide will explain the topic quicker and more comprehensively than for me to respond with my own written (or verbal) version.

I've seen excellent documentation, and I have seen terrible documentation. As I mention later, I like working on updating manuals and user's guides, but not for a living. While it's difficult to improve on an excellent document, overhauling documents of lesser quality can help make your job as a Help Desk Tech a lot less difficult.

There are times when documenting some event is just not appropriate. One example I experienced was the bright idea (not mine) of creating a video documenting the installation of a brand new version of an accounting application tailored specifically for the User. The concept was to save on support resources and put the responsibility upon the User to install the upgrade. The installation also included a requirement for running a conversion program since the database had also been restructured. Even as the manger of the support department, I couldn't convince the powers-that-be that this was not a good idea.

Sure enough, I received more phone calls and emails on how to install the video, view the video, pause, rewind, replay, slow it down, speed it up, than I ever received on just installing the application update itself! Needless to say, I went back to my previous method of scheduling times with each User, and had everyone personally assist with the installation. The personal interaction with each user early on in the release process ended up paying some nice dividends.

We were able to debug most of the conversion program and eliminate other anomalies saving the majority of our customer base the extra aggravation. I presented this one-on-one concept as a value added incentive to keep customers enrolled in our subscription support program. And, it's an excellent strategy to touch base with your customers; field any questions they may have, listen to suggestions for future upgrades, and don't forget: sell them on your contract support and any new modules they may need.

Newsletters

Newsletters are great if you can afford the time for the extra work. Newsletters can contain marketing information to push new products, updates, and services. They can include sections on new product enhancements, recent corrections to software errors, Knowledge Base articles, and Frequently Asked Questions.

Newsletters are a great vehicle to educate, and more often remind, users about the research tools on your website that compliment Help Desk Technical Support. I use newsletters to give pointers on how best to utilize existing documentation to answer the less complex questions. The concept is to take some pressure off of the support staff and lower call and email volume regarding support issues. I have found that quarterly newsletters with more quality content work better than monthly newsletters. For one thing, more time passes allowing for greater accumulation and sampling of customer calls and emails, software error corrections, and enhancements from which to choose from, which become the subjects of the newsletter itself.

Exporting

If the applications you support include export capabilities, then you have a powerful tool with which to educate your users to perform more complex problem solving on their own. An excellent example might be after a new record has been entered, yet the user is unable to find the new record by conventional methods. The user can export all pertinent records and pull the exported file into a spreadsheet. Search for, and subtotal by last name. Have you found it? If the first and last name were switched upon entry, then the answer is "no". Have the user search for the last name in the first name field. This example shows how the user can inadvertently reverse the entry of the first and last names of a new address record. If you think about it, it is a simple mistake but not necessarily an easy one to find. Impress upon the user on the power of the spreadsheet software itself. They have the ability to search, sort, and subtotal their exported data.

File Maintenance

This is an area that should be a no-brainer for even an entry level tech. Maintaining organization of files and folders is essential on any system primarily just to allow people to find things. For a software development firm, that means storing individual projects in its' own folder, groups of projects for a given major version should either be in a separate folder or even on another logical drive. This is basic stuff, common sense, yet I constantly see file organization, or lack thereof, that would put the most serious hoarder look like a clean freak.

Educating customers about file maintenance helps them help you in the long run. Application installations with consistent application and data location takes the guess work out of trying to find were everything is.

I'm assuming here that you may be supporting hundreds, perhaps thousands, of systems. Having a clue where stuff is saves time. I have run into a couple of cases where the user's local drive was something other than "C:". Although installing the OS on "E:" or "G:" is valid, I think it's inept.

I'd give a months' pay to know how some users manage to do it, but I've seen production data folders nested three deep (as in Q:\Data\Data\Data\Data), four if you count the fact the primary folder is shared on a network drive and mapped on all the workstations. This is obviously a precarious situation. In a concurrent user application, particularly in legacy applications, different users could be using different versions of what is supposed to be the same database. And unscrambling this mess can be a major headache as I have had to deal with it on a few occasions. Add this one to your repertoire of preventive strategies by taking a quick look at your user's databases whenever you have the opportunity.

One time I emptied a guy's Recycle Bin without asking him, and he definitely wasn't happy about it. Turns out that was one of his most important file management tools. From that time on, I always ask before emptying anybody's Recycle Bin.

FTP

When I send an FTP link, I always send a paragraph of instructions like this:

"Some browsers require the user to click the 'Page' button, followed by clicking 'Open FTP site in a Separate Browser Window', ('password' is the same for both the username and password in the event you are prompted). If you experience an error accessing this page, copy/paste the above link directly into the browser.

You may need to refresh the page (click F5, or click the Refresh button) if this page has been cached as a result of a prior download from this site.

Note: If you are having problems using FTP in a specific browser, please try a different browser."

Users can be denied access to FTP by their network administrators. When a user can't access your FTP site to upload their files, ask them to have their IT department upload the file since they have administrative credentials. If their IT department refuses to believe the problem is not their fault, ask your user to take the file and upload it from home.

I've been fortunate to have either maintained a remote session with the FTP server, or better yet, have the server in my office. Monitoring the FTP server allows me to track who is downloading or uploading what and when. From this, I can anticipate when to expect responses as a result. I can also see if the user is having any specific problems with the process. Then there are, of course, those who will needlessly download an installer I've made available for them – to every workstation they have, simultaneously. So much for bandwidth for a couple hours. Never underestimate the capabilities of any user.

I have found it's not unusual for an executable to get corrupted during an FTP session. The tell tale sign is a General Protection Fault when the executable is launched at the target location.

Get Closer to the Code

One area I haven't discussed which can be a valuable tool for quickly locating and correcting bugs is the ability to step through source code.

I have been privileged in the past to have the developer environment readily available for my use. Even though I have an extensive application programming background, any experience between entry and intermediate level coding should be enough to take advantage of this set of tools. In time, you may even get "intimate" with the code where you can make changes "on the fly". Since your knowledge of the system you are supporting is more from the user's standpoint, you are generally able to zero in on how a particular part of that system is supposed to work. Most of the time, this gives you an advantage over the programming staff as they see things strictly as code. I tend to locate a specific line of code that is failing, and make a recommendation to the programming staff as to what I think the correction should be and let them implement any changes. I would rather they remain responsible for maintaining sources.

I also like to save earlier complied versions, or builds, so I can go back and establish chronologically when a problem may have started happening. This is one more piece of information that can be used to collaborate with any comments in the code, assuming the programmers are energetic or competent enough to include a time stamp on the changes and additions they make.

Help from the User

This tactic should be unnecessary, and it's certainly unfortunate when I have no other choice. But there comes a time when a customer has been promised a perk and you've been waiting for management to give the green light to allow the programming department to implement it. And, they never seem to remember you reminding them about it recently.

Meanwhile, the customer is calling you whining about how long it's been and wants to know when it will finally be available. Simple solution: enlist the aid of the client to push your management.

I call the customer (don't email, I don't think your boss will be too impressed with this technique) and explain that I need him to help me help him. I ask the customer to send an email to the appropriate boss on my end. I suggest that he should be firm about it. If there is no response within a reasonable amount of time, I ask the customer to call. It's amazing how quickly management will move on an item when the customer inquires about it.

High Maintenance Users

Statistically, there will always be some number of users who consistently require more attention than those who I would refer to as otherwise "average". Some of the reasons might include inabilities to retain information, lack of organization, or perhaps these are clients actually utilizing the entire system and therefore apply more stress on your support resources, however unlikely.

What I have found to be more plausible is the fact that users are resistant to change, particularly when a user is upgraded from a legacy system to one which is more state-of-the-art. One question I've had to field constantly with new users is "I assume you wouldn't be in business if all of your users had the same problems as I do, so why am I having so many problems?". I still haven't figured out a tactful way of informing these users that they lack an upgrade of their own skills, or maybe worse.

Hours of Operation

During my tenure in various organizations located on the West Coast, one of the concerns that users in other time zones had was our hours of operation. Our hours of 8:30am PST to 5:30pm PST was not a big hit with east coast customers. And, in several cases, I offered my employer to stagger my shift to provide better coverage. It would have worked out great for me because of and easier commute, but for whatever reason I never could convince management. So, we do the best we can with the resources at hand. I ended up allocating the first four hours of the business day exclusively for east coast customers, and the last four hours for those in CST and PST. My response to users on this matter was that even though our office hours did not cover their entire working day, I did allocate more available time in their favor. When this issue becomes a concern for prospective clients, this response also works well as marketing tool.

Mom and Pop Shops

Small businesses without IT departments can either be a blessing or a nightmare, the bottom line is to use extreme care. Supporting network applications often requires assistance from the network administrator. It's great when there is one, but small shops usually outsource those requirements. It's nice when you can service a small shop by going above and beyond the call.

When servicing larger organizations, I do not touch anything without the express written consent of their IT department. Accessing a network beyond just a user's workstation is a liability issue, and one of respecting professional courtesy. Of course there may be extenuating circumstances that allows sensitive areas of a corporate LAN to be accessed by an outside vendor.

I suggest you obtain and carefully review your companies' policy with regards to servicing your customers' network. And, it's unlikely your subscription support includes performing the functions of a net administrator on a clients' network anyway.

Smaller shops are usually much more casual. And, they tend not to want to pay for a service call (which may not be an issue if they are paying a retainer). If you are qualified and comfortable, go ahead and access the server to confirm access rights, review the Event Viewer, or remap a local drive to a different shared folder. Beware however, if anything happens (and that includes anything that doesn't have anything to do with you or what you did or might have done) it will come back to bite you in the backside. And that is why I do not recommend servicing beyond the scope of what you are contractually obligated to provide.

One-Point-of-Contact

Support and maintenance contracts vary when addressing areas such as a limit on number of hours of support per year, entitlement to updates as opposed to upgrades, number of licensed users, and designated points of contact. I tend to overlook limitations on how much support any given user ends up getting. If management decides that too much support is being provided to a particular user, then something is obviously wrong. And it's one of two things: the user is not capable of performing the tasks of the position they hold, or whatever applications they are using don't work. It's that simple.

Upgrades differ from updates in the sense that the former is typically a chargeable event and the latter is usually offered as part of a support or maintenance agreement.

Since management is going to want the proceeds from purchases of upgrades, then it is not a good idea to give those away. Licensing is also another revenue generator, don't give those away.

One-Point-of-Contact is a rule that I do enforce. The first time you see three of four of your fellow help desk staff running around at the same time with the same problem from the same user, you'll figure it out. To compound things even more, things always get lost in translation to the point that the same problem now becomes several different perceived problems. I had (at least) one experience where a customer hired several consultants to act on their behalf, or as a "mediator", between them and my support department. This situation caused a tremendous strain on our resources as all of a sudden we're providing training and support to both their users and consultants.

Overseas Support (OMG)

My condolences if you MUST deal with an out sourced or off-shore support organization. Well, what's left to say about this topic? I do the best I can not to do business with any organization that forces you to call someplace 12,000 miles away, talk to someone who barely speaks English with a heavy accent (they often sound like they're sucking on a bag of marbles), is not even a Level I technician, and a crappy VoIP just to top things off.

I had one notable experience with such a support representative for which the above is a perfect definition. Basically I had switched ISP's at home (by the way, this happened to be perhaps the oldest, largest, and most well known of all phone companies) and had no Internet access upon installing the new modem. Well, how hard can that be to fix?

Believe me, I tried everything before having to make that dreaded call. I reset the modem, restarted the workstation, switched cables, tried different RJ11C's, and ran the modem diagnostics, no luck. Made the call, and she started down her to-do list. Which I understand, I had to be patient. Then she told me to insert a ball point pen into the little hole with a reset button on the bottom of the modem. There was NO hole on the bottom of the modem. She YELLED at me to find the hole on BOTTOM of the modem. I couldn't believe it! She screamed at me! Anyway, I found the hole on the SIDE of the modem conveniently hidden under a paper seal clearly marked "Do Not Remove", which I promptly removed. Long story short, I ended up talking to a technician in St. Louis, who dispatched a technician to my home. The problem turned out to be the modem configuration was wrong for the type of connection between my house and the B-Box. The time between initial failed install and repair was eleven days. I made the telephone company credit me for that downtime.

So, if you're one of those unfortunates who don't have a choice, here are a couple of tips that might help:

Anytime you get someone who is rude, can't understand, or they're an idiot, hang up and call back. Repeat until you get someone you can deal with.

Then, if you're not getting anywhere fast, make things as difficult for him as possible. You're an experienced tech, start by being overly helpful. Inquire about lost lease on the IP (or whatever technical stuff applies that you know he can't handle). I pulled this one off in the past with a Telco when my Internet access failed. If being over helpful doesn't work, reverse course and make like a moron. It'll take more time, but when I've had to resort to these techniques, I'd at least get to talk to a level II tech on indigenous soil.

Process of Elimination (PoE)

Also known as a brute force tactic, PoE can be very effective when tracking down a problem. The following is a true story which illustrates the elegance of PoE.

I figure you have to have at least one nightmare every other month or so just to keep you sharp. The first nightmare I had while employed as a Help Desk Tech at a small software development firm involved bringing up a third workstation for a client running our applications, which were also based on a well known relational database engine. The installation was successful, services were running prior to launching the app, but upon launch, the app failed every time. I tried reinstalling as an administrator, shutting off the firewall, disabling the antivirus software, all of the things on my list. And still could not get this third workstation up. I analyzed the other two workstations that were operational for any clues. After a week or so of trying various things, I decided to start removing other applications, one at a time. The first application I removed was the antivirus and software firewall manufactured by one of the most well known companies who specialize in the industry. Bingo! Everything started working. What had happened was the antivirus and firewall software was shutting down the relational database services without any kind of error or informative message. You'll recall I did disable this app as part of my troubleshoot, but disabling obviously wasn't enough. Unbelievable!

A month or so after starting a new position as a Help Desk Tech at a small software publishing company, I found out that our servers had never functioned properly since they were purchased about a year and a half prior. I asked if I could take a look, but as a new employee, it took another month or so before they were comfortable with me.

17

Turns out, they had never been able to utilize the tape backup, none of the browsers would function, antivirus had never been operational, and the server took several hours to restart. I searched the web for clues based on these symptoms, granted they are broad, but after a couple of days in between support calls, I found an obscure article about a software upgrade that was released about a year and a half prior for the UPS. The article went on to mention all of the symptoms, and pointed me to the appropriate upgrade.

As soon as I removed the UPS software, to my total astonishment, without even restarting the servers, everything just started working! The boss didn't believe me at first. But, he quit docking my pay for time off for doctor and dentist after he realized I had actually fixed something that several consultants, techs from the hardware vendor, and his own staff, were unable to resolve.

To summarize, when encountering problems of this magnitude, I like the simple approach of removing suspect applications that may conflict with what you are trying to support. In my previous story, I was actually surprised that nobody thought to just wipe the drives and start all over, but that's not always the best option either. I supposed that had they done that, they would have installed the same version of software to support the UPS that caused all of the issues in the first place.

Remote Access

Remote access is a topic that you will get hit with by your customers often. They're going to want to know if and how your applications work with various environments that require users to access those applications from remote locations. My brief discussion is suitable for responding to that initial inquiry.

Remote Access is a term that describes the ability to access a workstation and/or server on a network from a location that physically resides away from the corporate location. An excellent example of a use of Remote Access is the fact that my office workstation is always connected via one of those commercial PC to PC communication apps. This gives me the ability to provide email support, PC to PC communication support, and other company related functions from my home in the event I am unable to get to my office. There are three layers of security which must be addressed for me to gain access to my office workstation. First, a username and password must be entered to get into the PC to PC communication app. Second, an access code must be entered to enable the connection from the remote location to gain access to my office workstation. Third, I must authenticate myself on the corporate network by logging in with a valid username and password.

There are many options available in addition to the PC to PC communication app that I use. But, many of those options are far more expensive, require maintenance, and are difficult to use, yet they don't necessarily provide any additional security or functionality. I use this particular app to service my users because it is relatively inexpensive, reliable, and easy to use. I also set the PC to PC app as the default home page in my browser since I use it a lot. It also looks good to the boss should he walk into your office and want to show you something on the web. Regardless of the remote access method that is selected, the concept stays the same - you have a user outside the corporate network that gains access to that network, and appropriate security measures must be evaluated.

Now that you have recommended options for Remote Access, you need to educate them about the bad news.

The remote user may experience resolution issues, and will definitely squawk about latency because of bandwidth limitations. Let them know ahead of time so you don't catch the flak later. One more tip, I never drag and drop anything while connected to another machine. Always copy and paste thereby reducing the chances of clobbering somebody's files or rearranging their desktop.

Reports, Reconciliation, and Rounding

If you support applications that are report intensive, and most are, I suggest preparing for questions about each and every column, row, heading, total, and grand total on every report in the system. If your User's Guide is up-to-date and describes all reports in the level of detail I just described, and you understand it to the point of being able to explain it to any user, I say congratulations! You're at least a Level III tech.

If your User's Guide is not up-to-date or simply doesn't have descriptions of what the report content is, I say you're going to be quite busy for awhile. Many systems I've supported include a single page description of each report then assume the user is going to know the rest. Problems arise with differences in terminology within the same industry, and even if everyone involved has some basic knowledge of General Ledger concepts, it's highly unlikely everyone will agree on how every report is to be calculated. The use of different accounting principles, and rounding, can contribute to differences between reports from a legacy application and a state-of-the-art commercially available application.

Reports become a huge issue particularly after a conversion from old system to new system. The client wants reports from the new system to reconcile to the penny to those on the old system.

Obviously, this is not an unrealistic request when it involves cash balances, accounts receivables, and accounts payables. Other numbers, such as cash projections, are virtually impossible to reconcile. How do you know how this was calculated on the old system (of which the vendor no longer exists even if you could ask the question)? The best you can do is establish an acceptable ballpark for margin for error of maybe a fraction of a percent and except the fact that 64 bit is going to be more accurate than 16 bit and move on.

One of the more challenging concepts I've had to educate a user on is "static" reports generated as a result of a month-end close versus looking at data generated by the system in real-time. Explaining how dynamic data will not reconcile with a report generated days or weeks ago because today's data simply isn't the same as that of the last close can be frustrating at best. Even more frustrating is having to explain why two different reports in the same system will not reconcile.

Granted, there may be more than one report in a system containing the same calculated data which will reconcile, but it's likely for purposes of presentation. Because accountants want to see the same numbers from two different reports, I've had to explain on many occasions there are not two different reports from the same system reporting the same calculated data. What would be the purpose? And, if there were two separate reports, they would both be generated from the same data source anyway.

This one is fun, because I directed the effort right at the source of contention. The argument was how to compute total sales tax. The programming department I had to liaison with at the time couldn't understand why the user complained about an incorrect total sales tax amount.

The simple solution I offered was to round the sales tax amount from each record before cumulating and round the total. They didn't believe it until they changed the code from just cumulating without rounding. Sometimes you have to get a little insistent when you know you're right. Besides, I had already proved it with the user's real data.

A number of years ago I supported products designed for the financial services industry, mainly portfolio accounting for stocks, bonds, and other types of securities. I'm still amazed, and I'm not sure if the industry has since changed, there were no standards for rounding. While some financial institutions rounded at three, four, six, or even eight digits, others simply truncating at three. Compound this with applying exchange rates when trading currencies or other securities, and you have a reconciliation nightmare between systems.

Yet another scenario, I was responsible for maintaining a large spreadsheet with perhaps thirty or more separate worksheets for tracking company sales and commissions broken down by product and territory. Virtually every cell had a relation to another cell which had a relation to another cell, and so on. The problem before I arrived on the scene was they could never get it to reconcile, and everything had to reconcile to the penny, no kidding. Similar to the sales tax event I described earlier, I suggested adding rounding to every cell in the spreadsheet. Naturally, there was disbelief this could solve the problem. Unfortunately, I was the one chosen for the task of making thousands of changes to the formulas. But when all was said and done, it always reconciled to the penny thereafter.

Screen Shots

I insist users email how ever many screen shots it takes to describe a specific problem or inquiry adequately before they pick up the phone. The screen shot(s) should contain the error message, informative message, or related area the inquiry is regarding, captured along with the entire screen. This allows you to see exactly where in the application the user is describing, and with any luck, what the precise problem or question really is. The screen shot(s) should include two or three sentences detailing the circumstances of the error, or a precisely stated question. You can't work with just "we have a problem".

Screen shots are an invaluable tool for a variety of reasons. Screen shots generally give you some idea of what the issue is before you have to spend time on the phone. Many times, if the problem is recognized as resolved by a previous ticket, an updated application can be sent to the user. I'd like to have a buck for every time a user types (or rather, mistypes) the error message in an email with no screen shot, only to never be able to reproduce it again and not know what the problem really was. Educating users to email their questions and problems saves time and reduces the phone bill. In many cases, the problem is resolved quicker. If you are located on the west coast, your east coast users can often have an answer first thing their next morning. Another tool is to have the user email questions or problems regarding a report by printing the report to a PDF file, annotate if appropriate, and email the PDF. Faxed reports are usually illegible by the time they get to you. However, you may not have a choice if the printed material in question originated at from a legacy app that doesn't support printing to PDF. I also try to discourage scanning such material into a PDF, again, it is usually unreadable by the time I receive it. The only reliable way to obtain such printed material, unfortunately, is by snail mail.

Screen shots work wonderfully when the situation is reversed. For example, you can email an annotated screen shot back to the user showing exactly where or what a specific field is for. I respond by phone and online connection as a last resort. Quite simply, if emailing back and forth to resolve an issue takes longer than it took me to write the paragraph above, then call and connect. Your customer is your bread and butter, you must keep them happy. Plus, it's far less unpleasant dealing with a user that's not already reached some level of aggravation.

Every time you connect with a user, always backup their data before performing any trouble shooting. And, never trust them if they tell you it's already been backed up. I'm here to tell you, if so much as a bit is dropped, they'll come right back to you.

Setting Up Test Cases – Regression Testing

Fixing bugs in an application is only part of the process. Duplicating a problem to begin with is a whole other story.

The programmer will be "stepping through" source code to locate where the app is failing. The better you can isolate where in the application the failure is occurring, the less stepping he has to do. By duplicating the problem in-house often zeros in on a specific routine saving the programmer considerable time debugging. If you support a commercial application, then you are getting the problem reported by a customer. They will send you a screen shot and a brief description of the how, when, and where. Depending on the complexity of the app, there may be many different approaches that can be taken to get to the same location of the error. Only one of which actually causes the failure.

Your job is to narrow it down to the specific set of key strokes and mouse clicks that reproduces the problem. And, the smaller the test case, the better. If you are unable to reproduce the error with a test case means one to two things: you are not duplicating exactly what the user did, or the problem is data related. Resilience is the key if you're unable to reproduce the problem by setting up a test case, if it is data related, you'll likely have to get the customer's data.

In the event the problem is data related, make sure you have researched all of the tools available to repair any files that might be a part of a commercial database application. Many tools will allow rebuilding of files which sometimes can recover a corrupted record. Other tools will include options to export a binary file to sequential, followed by importing the sequential file back to a clone (empty) binary file of the same format, again possibly recovering a corrupted record.

Tip: Ask your programmers to make a backup of the project locally before making changes. If, for any reason, you need to restore back to the original copy, it saves the IT department (probably you) from having to drop everything to restore from backup media. And, it's likely they'll trash the thing again anyway. The same applies to databases, both production databases that might have been uploaded by the customer and in-house test databases. Back them up by simply making a copy. That way, you can easily restore back to the original form if you have to retest a bug fix.

Shipping Media

Sometimes it makes sense to burn a DVD and drop it in snail mail rather than trying to FTP if you're dealing with a large database.

Large files can take hours to upload, and the larger the file, the better the chances of a connection failure during the transfer. Then you have to start all over. Anytime I request data on media such as a DVD, I always ask that two copies be sent. I can't tell you how many times I have received a DVD only to have it fail when trying to read it. I also instruct the user to place the DVD in a jewel case and mail it in a DVD mailer, which is basically a cardboard envelope.

I have received DVD's loose in a standard envelope, and thumb drives loose in a small box. I am always amazed at the lack of common sense of anyone who can't think to appropriately pack such fragile items. Major carriers do post packaging recommendations such as the ability to withstand the impact of another package weighing 70 lbs from a height of three feet. And, they don't hand carry a package just because it has "FRAGILE" plastered all over it. If anything, the larger the word "FRAGILE", the harder it's going to get thrown. I know this from personal experience.

Tighter Security, Protecting You From Yourself

Operating systems, Networks, and Email Servers are becoming ever more secure. While justified, it does make your job that much more challenging. If there is any doubt that a problem might be caused because of a failed installation, reinstall either by running the installer as an administrator, or log in to the workstation as a domain administrator (literally log in as "administrator") with domain administrator credentials.

Triage

Priority must be assigned based on the severity of the problem. A customer who is completely down and is unable to conduct business must be given the highest priority. Other high priorities include resolving issues for which a workaround has been deployed, installation of updates or upgrades, and fielding specific questions regarding the application. Low priorities might include correction of minor software issues and repair of cosmetic problems. If you have to re-schedule an appointment with a customer to direct resources to a higher priority and that customer complains, simply remind them you would do the same for them.

Most of the time (hopefully) open tickets will all be low priority issues. I recommend, if possible, resolving the least difficult issues first. Keep as many customers as possible happy in the shortest length of time. However, it's been my experience where there are usually many high priority issues are occurring simultaneously. Then priority goes to whoever is screaming the loudest.

Trouble Shooting

Anytime a user reports a problem, make available the latest release version (and even the latest beta version) of the application to confirm the problem still exists. Always troubleshoot the latest version of the application.

One technique that works occasionally, particularly with "problem users", is to give them an extended period of time prior to following up. By the time you contact them for details regarding the "problem" they've reported, they likely have resolved it on their own.

Ask as Many Questions as You Want

The first task when troubleshooting a problem is to clearly define the problem. Now you become sort of a CSI agent, you have to ask a lot of questions. And the user not only isn't going to be happy about it, but he's also not likely to be overly cooperative.

Examples: When did you install the last update? What antivirus software do you currently have installed? Is this a new workstation? What changes have been made to the network since the last update? I cover more appropriate questions for specific issues elsewhere in this guide. The point I want to make here is not to be shy about asking questions regardless of what the user deems appropriate. Determining a pattern, whether chronological, a certain piece of hardware, or a specific user, is key to resolving chronic problems that otherwise cannot be reproduced at will. As I've pointed our before, if they know more about the problem and how to resolve it, then why did they call you in the first place?

Mind Reading

Why do so many people think you can read their minds? Here is a typical example of a question for which you are supposed to provide the correct detailed answer: "One of our customers is reducing the number of copies he is purchasing, what's the best way to handle this?" Now, I'm pretty sure he wants to know how to apply the credit for the reduction in purchased product to a future purchase.

But since this is the third time I have asked for more detail, I have decided to give an exact answer to his exact question: "Change the number of copies".

When I run across this type of user, I don't waste my time trying to educate them on how to ask simple questions. This response technique won't make you a hero, but it will soon teach this type of user how to better communicate, unfortunately the hard way.

Unsupported Customers

I sympathize for those affected by economic conditions. However, you wouldn't cancel collision insurance on a vehicle with a couple years of payments left when instead you could forego your annual cruise this year and go camping instead. If you total the uninsured vehicle, you lose. And a fine restaurant wouldn't compromise quality or significantly reduce portions on the very product that keeps them in business. Those that do will go out of business. There is absolutely no excuse for this type of business behavior.

Your customers that don't stay current on their subscription maintenance to software applications and hardware warranties place themselves at the same level of risk. When they go down for any reason, they jeopardize their only resource – their customers. This is an excellent example of *penny wise and pound foolish*. The usual excuse for not maintaining a support contract offered by the customer usually revolves around the fact that since they have had no problems within the last 6 months or a year, how can they justify the cost of renewing? Of course, when the unsupported user calls with a crisis, renews their expired support contract on the spot, they expect you to drop everything at a moment's notice. They don't understand the concept that you actually have other paying customers who have consistently maintained their subscription maintenance. And, while this is certainly unfair, cash flow must be considered a priority as well.

I would at least charge a penalty fee for the wing nuts who don't keep their subscription maintenance current.

The irony in most cases, as it turns out, the unsupported customer has already spent three or four times the renewal amount, not to mention the week of down time, for an outside IT consultant to try to solve the problem. Then I come in and get them up and running in an hour or two. Makes sense to me.

When an unsupported customer calls for support, it's usually a delicate situation, now what? Depending on your company policy, there are several techniques for handling this circumstance. First and foremost, you want them to re-up on their support contract. If they are behind on updates or upgrades, you will want to pursue any update or upgrade fees that apply. You can expect the typical response from the unsupported customer: "but we've been using your product for fifteen years and we've *almost* never called for anything". Get out the violin. And then inquire as to how many widgets they've given away for the past fifteen years at no charge. Free doesn't pay the bills, and it doesn't justify the boss' signature on your paycheck. It's that simple.

If the unsupported customer doesn't want to subscribe to annual support, they may ask if there is an hourly charge. Again, depending on your company policy, that is probably an option. My experience has been to quote the hourly charge and state a minimum of at least two hours. This hourly charge should apply as a one-time event, it doesn't cover any other events related or not. The point I make to the unsupported customer in all this is, why not just re-up on their subscription maintenance contract?

By the time you're done with hourly rates getting their problems solved (and maybe you can't because they are running a five or ten year old version of the application because they have never paid to upgrade), they've practically paid for the annual support contract.

The other half of this delicate situation is the fact the boss absolutely, positively, under no circumstances, will allow you to provide any service to an unsupported customer. The problem I have with this is typically by the time you find out exactly what the problem is, you've ended up resolving it in the process for free. The unsupported customer remains unsupported, no check in the mail, and the boss is asking why. I will argue there must be a strict policy that you do not discuss any problems or solutions unless the customer has made appropriate arrangements with your boss.

Here's one excuse for the record:

I once had an unsupported customer call for technical assistance. I referred her to the appropriate department to renew her subscription. She actually argued that she needed help but couldn't afford it because she and her husband had just returned from two weeks in Paris. I swear, I don't make this stuff up.

Upgrades and Updates

The difference between an upgrade and an update is usually defined by whether the new version represents a new generation of software applications rather than a series of patches to an existing version. Version numbers such as 7.0, 8.0, and 9.0 usually represent a new Upgrade which may require a re-install, data conversion, or other special instructions.

Version numbers such as 7.1, 8.1, and 9.1 often refer to a set of patches that constitute an update to the previous upgrade. While this is a simple example, builds work basically the same way. It's a matter of how Product Development managers want to handle one aspect of version control. It's not unusual in smaller organizations version control that relies solely on the date and time stamp of the application. But relying on OS date and time stamps gets dicey because the stamps get changed, for example, upon downloading via FTP.

Custom Applications (are an Administrative Nightmare)

They don't have to be though. But, how many times have you generated a major upgrade to the flagship product only to find that about fifty custom reports and features were left out? And, of course, you find out about this via fifty not so pleasant phone calls from customers. Yes, the obvious solution is a tracking system that includes everything each customer has. But I have discussed tracking systems, and no matter what they are used for, they are only as good as those that use them and are adamant about maintaining them. All it takes is one member of the staff (usually the department manager) who lacks consistent cooperation, and you have a failed tracking system.

As a former Manager of Product Development, my solution to this problem was quite simple: all custom code becomes part of the general release application, no exceptions. It would then be difficult to miss custom reports and features during both the development process and upgrade. The key to this technique is to build a simple licensing system which controls access to a given custom report or feature. And that's only if you care, because you're right back to if the license is incorrectly configured, you're going to get the ugly call from the user.

At least it's just a matter of sending a new license file. My philosophy is to maintain a completely open system. The likelihood of anyone using a custom report designed for a specific user is slim. It's even less likely if your management decides to go the license route because their intention is to sell the custom report.

Note: I'd like to have a buck for every time a user tells me how many more sales I could make if I could just add this one feature or report. The user, of course, is pleading his case to get what he wants for free. When customers start complaining about how much they pay for subscription support, and that it should include custom product development, my standard response is "Mr. Johnson, how many of your Widgets to you give away for free each month?". If that doesn't put things into perspective, then I continue with "Mr. Johnson, the supermarket doesn't give me the groceries to feed my family away for free."

When to Send Updates, Upgrades

Assuming you are supporting niche applications and incur revenue from annual maintenance and/or support contracts, I highly recommend scheduling delivery of a set of update CD's several months prior to invoice for next years' support fee. This approach gives the user something physical to put their hands on, a feat obviously difficult to do with software. I tend to include a separate CD, each with its' own specific application installation and any relevant documentation, including a list of changes and bug fixes (I refer to bug fixes as "software corrections" The "B" word is already way overused, try to avoid it). If possible, send an updated hard copy of the User's Guide along with each pertinent CD. This is a good marketing ploy, as these are inexpensive incentives that encourage the customer to renew their maintenance.

This is an excellent tool to offer as another "value added" piece that compliments the product and you are demonstrating the fact that you haven't forgotten about them as a valued client.

Other value added incentives might include offering to schedule a session to perform the installation of the update for the user, review the user's file maintenance relevant to the product you are supporting (as in clean up files from old versions of the app that are obsolete), an informal tutorial on the latest changes and additions to the latest version of the app, and perhaps a "tune-up" which may include a review of how the customer might take further advantage of new and existing features to improve productivity.

Tip: Always address any correspondence directly to whoever signs the checks.

Sending Releases

Although there are numerous vehicles than can be used to deliver updates and upgrades, my focus here assumes you manage this task at a smaller niche software company. This is the environment I am most accustomed to. A smaller customer base whereby each customer must be individually configured based on the specific modules, custom applications and licensing requirements often takes more care and time than just pushing patches over the Internet.

I recommend sending the installers which include any patches and updates. I also recommend sending any third party applications that you are licensed to distribute even though they are not necessary for purposes of installing the updates in support of your application.

The point being, if you don't, someone is going to call needing a complete re-install and, of course, they don't have a complete set of CD's.

Application Evolution

Newer versions of applications tend to be more sensitive to problems caused by bugs in previous and legacy versions. An excellent example might be certain bytes in the records of a customer name and address file may not have been initialized in an older version of the app. A new version of the app may fail if it expects those fields in the records to be zeroed instead of just null or random values, aka garbage.

Version Stabilization

Experience has shown me that as a new version of an application stabilizes, bug reports get far more complex and detailed. The initial release of an upgrade after beta is always going to have "major" bugs. The good news is that major bugs tend to be easier to reproduce and correct, and most of that phase should be gone by the next update. The not so good news is as users begin to take advantage of the more obscure features and options, and find bugs, the greater the challenge becomes for the support team to locate, reproduce, and identify those issues. It would be wise to plan ahead for this possibility.

You're Not a Politician, Don't Sugar Coat It

There is no such thing as bug-free software or systems. I am often asked prior to installing and update or upgrade: "What kind of problems should we expect us to have?", my response is "None, but I won't guarantee it.".

I would rather be up front with a customer and let them know that nothing is out of the realm of possibility rather than to have to answer to them if and when something bad does happen. There have been plenty of times when major software manufacturers released an update that brought down entire corporate networks.

Fortunately, for me anyway, the worst I have had to deal with were issues caused by older versions of the application. During the evolution of an application, bugs are fixed, more data gets validated, and the system continues to stabilize. That's all well and good, but that means newer versions of the application are going to be less forgiving of problems caused by the earlier versions.

Using Search Engines

Even though the most entry level of techs knows to use search engines as a matter of routine, I discuss the subject anyway because it's such a valuable tool. I remember being connected and troubleshooting a problem for a customer when I needed to bring up the Task Manager. Because the client machine had an older OS, there was no button on my connection application available to send a Ctrl-Alt-Del. I searched for an alternative, and what do you know! Turns out, clicking on Start to display the Start Menu and typing Shift-Ctrl-Esc at the same time launches the Task Manger on the remote machine. Kind' a handy. And, virtually any Windows operation can be done from the Command Prompt.

If you are having trouble finding info on some technical issue like an error message on your favorite search engine, try a different search engine. Often times a search on a different engine will yield different results, and hopefully find your answer.

Winging It

Sometimes, maybe most of the time, when troubleshooting a new application or something on the network, you just have to fool with it. Fly by the seat of your pants and don't be afraid to make changes to determine effect. As long as data is backed up the only thing you might lose is having to reinstall whatever it is you're tinkering with. One example is when I've had problems sending and/or receiving email. The worst case scenario (WCS) is to reinstall the email server applications which, as you know, is a nightmare. I would rather fool with restarting services, dismount then remount the store, or simply restart the server before considering a complete reinstall. This might not be a great example because there are so many factors regarding email failure. A better example of what I am describing is how I (sort of) taught my eleven year old daughter to use a word processor. I started by tutoring her with the basics. Once she became fluent with the keyboard and basic navigation, she began to find all of the other tools. Naturally, flurries of questions about how to use obscure features I hadn't even known exist were hurled mercilessly at me non-stop. The solution was to tell her to fool with them, make her learn on her own. If you've invested considerable time figuring something out on your own, I guarantee you're less likely to forget it, whereas unlike a formal classroom environment where somebody is there to tell you how to do it.

And that's one difference between formal education and the real world. You can be a career student and never come close to gaining the type of education that comes with surviving outside the classroom. By the way, I have nothing against formal education. I am merely just pointing out the contrast between formal education and real world applications of your trade. This is why most potential employers want some combination of both.

The old Chinese proverb "Give a man a fish, feed him for a day. Teach a man to fish, feed him for a lifetime" is an appropriate analogy I use frequently to describe many of my support techniques.

Chapter 3 Technical Support, Training, and Maintenance

Technical Support vs. Training

Many organizations provide both technical support and training for their line of software products. Technical Support is often times a subscription based service purchased annually by the licensee and allows the licensee access to that organization's support technicians for the purpose of providing solutions to technical issues. Training is generally a scheduled and structured event specifically intended to provide personalized instruction of the use of that organization's software applications.

Technical issues may be defined (but necessarily limited to) by the following examples:

1) Assist with the installation of software applications on computers due to hardware or software [operating system] upgrades and/or malfunction.
2) Assist with diagnosis of workstation, server, and/or network issues with regards to the installation or operation of your company's software products.
3) Assist with operational issues, for example, the physical printing of reports, educating the user on the use of the products' user's guides, and the actual deployment of software applications.
4) In the event of a malfunction in the design or operation of the organization's products, Technical Support will assist the Licensee by defining the specific issue and ultimately submit the issue to the appropriate department within the organization for review and resolution.

The organization will make the resolved issue available to the licensee upon completion.

5) An organization's Technical Support department may, depending upon content, provide assistance with specific questions regarding the operation of it's' software applications. This assistance will usually result with a referral to a specific area in the appropriate User's Guide, typically a page number or chapter. Additional direction may be provided if the topic is not covered in the User's Guide, or other existing documents, for example, web based Knowledge Base articles or FAQ's.

6) Organization's Technical Support department typically does not provide training as defined later.

7) Organization's Technical Support department typically does not provide support or training for third party software applications (except as they may apply to documented topics in the User's Guide), operating systems, or network configuration or administration.

Defining Training, Support, and Maintenance

My definition of a trainer is a member of the technical staff that has experience in both a classroom environment and tutoring individuals. The trainer also possesses broad experience within the industry within which the application is designed to support. The trainer must be able to provide guidelines for a business model that fits the new customer's business with the application. My definition of training is a trainer that provides his undivided attention for an extended period of time for purposes of flattening the learning curve. Support is defined as addressing any and all problems associated with the systems and products provided by the vendor to the customer. I believe support should include the occasional question that might otherwise fall under the category of training as a value added incentive.

Maintenance is providing periodic upgrades or updates as a value added incentive to the customer to ensure the preservation of the business relationship. In short, you want the customer to continue to subscribe to support and maintenance contracts.

Training may be defined as follows:

The companies' authorized trainer provides undivided attention for an extended period of time for the purposes of educating users in both initial and ongoing operation of your companies' software product line. There are two types of training schedules that are typically offered:

Onsite Training offered at a fixed rate per day plus expenses. The authorized trainer arrives at the licensee site for eight hours of training. Multiple days may be purchased, however, onsite training is typically scheduled for a minimum of two days (two day minimum required), and a follow-up training session is scheduled anywhere from 6 to 8 weeks from the initial session.

On-Line Training is a fixed rate per hour. The authorized trainer connects into a user's workstation via a PC to PC communications application and is simultaneously in phone contact. The trainer has full keyboard and mouse control of the user's workstation, allowing the trainer to navigate through the companies' software application for purposes of providing training similar to that of onsite training without having to physically travel to the licensee site. On-Line Training is typically purchased in blocks of hours (there should be a minimum number of hours required), with follow up sessions scheduled as necessary.

Training can be provided in the form of refresher courses (beginner, intermediate, and advanced), or training can be tailored to target specific areas within the application (an excellent example might be importing and exporting data). Most commonly, training is provided in the event of personnel turnover. I recommend that users compose an itinerary prior to the training session which includes specific questions and/or topics within the applications on which training is desired. This itinerary can be provided in advance to the trainer to give him an opportunity to plan for a specific training session. Appendix E is an example of a course outline which is suitable for providing training to in-house personnel.

Chapter 4 Time Management and Organization

In this chapter I cover a few tips that help me better manage my time, stay organized, and reduce potential mistakes made when performing ordinary tasks.

I like to place the Recycle Bin icon behind an open folder of shortcut icons on my desktop to prevent accidental deletion of files when dragging. I use shortcut icons grouped in folders on my desktop primarily for those applications I use the most. I save the locations of more obscure applications and projects in my browser Favorites. These are usually the custom applications that you won't hear about for a few years, but when there is a problem or request for change, at least you'll have a fighting chance of finding them for the programming department. Likely nobody else is documenting stuff like this.

When connected remotely to a users' workstation and I have to push an updated file over, I usually use the file transfer option rather than dragging and dropping any files. I have inadvertently clobbered files and folders on the users' desktop when trying to drag and drop a file. If the users' desktop is heavily populated with files and folders, you also risk dropping your update into some folder, and then try to find it. Remember that you will be held accountable for any problems that occur after your session regardless of whether you were the cause. The idea is simply to reduce the margin for error.

One of the tasks I perform frequently for users is house cleaning. This is nothing more than deleting old or unnecessary files in the applications and data folders for the applications I support. Always backup all folders and files you plan to update or delete prior to beginning a purge. I've seen this lesson learned the hard way on more than one occasion.

Even though the user shouldn't store their documents, spreadsheets, or text files in the application installation or application data folders, you're still responsible if you delete files which haven't been backed up – and never assume the user has done so. Deleting files from Windows can be cumbersome. One trick is to go to the Command Line Prompt (CMD) and delete as many files as possible by the extension, for example: "del *.tmp". This method is quick and easy, but be careful, the deleted files don't go to the Recycle Bin, once they're gone, they are gone.

Having problems sending or receiving email? I always have a personal email account to test incoming and outgoing corporate email. Using an internal email address to test the corporate email server is ineffective because the email will not actually make it outside of the corporate LAN. I also use my outside email address to test a customer's email server if they are having problems. This is also part of CYB, or "Cover Your Backside",. If you are accused of not responding to an email inquiry because you never received it, this technique may help resolve whose email actually doesn't work.

Most of the problems I've encountered with software installations on corporate LAN's are due to access rights and permissions defined by the IT department on the users' side. I understand the concept of a secure LAN, however, I have seen series of groups containing different combinations of users each defined with different permissions and access rights. My experience with corporate IT departments says "you are highly unlikely to convince a corporate IT department that they have screwed up this whole issue of security so bad, you are unable to successfully deploy the application you are responsible for supporting".

Two simple tests from the users' workstation you must perform before approaching corporate IT: 1) Test access rights and permissions by attempting to create a simple text file on the server, open it, type something into it, save it. If it fails, you have your proof. 2) Browse to the location in question via Network Places. If that fails, they can't question your application because it's the OS.

I maintain a set of records in addition to any formal tracking systems or documentation procedures for events that are not corrected by the usual means. For example, an old version of a database engine that was not properly uninstalled prior to upgrading with a new version ends up causing data corruption or hard application errors. Another example might be certain configurations that unless done just right cause application failure. I'm describing situations that are usually out of the normal realm of Help Desk support. Events that tend to fall through the cracks when submitted to the next link in the chain. If an obscure event occurs at a customer site again, I have a chance at locating within my own documentation for the fix I applied on the previous occasion.

Never leave applications, spreadsheets, or other files open while you're away from your workstation. The programming department might be trying to recompile an application you have open. And, you risk losing work in progress in the event of a power failure or if the network goes down for any reason. Always save your work at reasonable intervals because auto-save features don't always work and UPS's do fail.

Here's a reason to close every application before installing anything: I've been embarrassed by the old screen behind screen bit I don't know how many times. You know what I'm talking about? Yup, it's when you're trying to install something and seemingly nothing is happening.

After wasting fifteen or twenty minutes you realize the installer has thrown up a window with the next prompt *behind* the window of another application. One would think the active application would have priority, in this case the installer, but unfortunately not always so.

Don't leave piles of documents or other media precariously close to the real recycle bin (the trash can). This one I have learned the hard way. Even though I couldn't prove it, I suspect the cleaning crew inadvertently knocked a few files from the edge of my desk into the circular, never to be seen again.

I never cut and paste, I copy and paste, then delete the unwanted copy. This applies primarily to very large files. I have lost files during a cut and paste due to network failure.

As mentioned elsewhere, I use connection applications much of the time to resolve support issues on the users' workstation. As you can believe, sometimes it takes more time to get connected than to resolve the support issue. And if the reason is not because of networking or Internet problems, it's operator error. Some users, for whatever reason, need seven or eight tries entering an email address and password to get you connected. Here's where I break one of my most reverent of rules: simplify the login as much as possible, for example, "remote@wigets.com". Use something like "abcd1234" for the access code. Most connection applications allow about three tries before shutting down for some period of time. If you use login Id's or access codes any more complex than my examples, prepare to waste a lot of time. Because I use such simple access codes, I make sure I have completely disconnected the user after each session, no exceptions.

Chapter 5 Email, a Powerful Management Tool

A Few Tips about Email

Ever send an email before you were actually finished with it? Of course you have. Take it from me, Mr. LARGE FOOT in even LARGER MOUTH, one inappropriate email can cost you your job!

I would suggest simply NOT entering the recipient's email address in the Send To field until you are absolutely sure you are ready to send the completed correspondence. This works okay for new emails, but what about responses? Again, perhaps not elegant, but delete the recipients email address until you are finished with your response. Take time to check spelling and grammar. And don't forget to attach the file you said you would. Temporarily erasing the recipient's email address also helps ensure that you are cognizant of whether you want to Reply To All, or to additional specific recipients. As I have mentioned previously, I tend to enforce one-point-of-contact and therefore never Reply To All. It doesn't take very long for too many cooks in the kitchen if everybody gets involved with someone's hang nail. When emailing a response, always assume the recipient might forward or respond back to someone else, like your boss – be careful what you say. The only time I ever use BCC is to send a copy of the email to myself for future reference. When sending an attachment, like an ".exe" that you've renamed to ".jpg" to bypass security issues, send a separate email letting the recipient know in case the attachment isn't received.

Acknowledging Your Mistakes

Always be truthful and accept the consequences for the mistakes you make. You will be respected for owning up, and besides, it's difficult to get away with anything in this digital age. I recall an experience I had with a TS'er (see Profiles) who blatantly changed the error logs and denied doing so even after the network log file was shown to her. The error logs she changed were part of an honor system to record one's mistakes solely for the purpose of maintaining ISO audit compliance. These logs had no impact on anyone's job performance and were not tied in anyway to the HR department. Evidently, she was unwilling to accept that fact and as a result was written up for unauthorized malicious tampering with corporate data. I don't recall how many days she was expelled from work without pay.

Auto Responder

Phone greetings and replies by Auto Responders should be detailed to the extent of the exact schedule of your absence, but be short and concise. An alternate should always be referenced in the event the customer has a "crisis":

"Hi, this is Dave in the Technical Support department. I will be out of the office Monday July 19, 2010 through Friday July 23, 2010. I will be back in the office Monday July, 26 2010 at 8:30a PST. If you require immediate assistance, please call Jim at extension 110. Please leave a message after the tone. Thank you."

Delivery of Service Guidelines

My goal as a Help Desk Tech is to respond within one business day with a solution, workaround, or an answer, but at very least, acknowledging receipt of the customer's inquiry.

In the event a user has a problem and before he knee-jerks by immediately picking up the phone to call you, I offer the user my general guideline when a problem is perceived. In the interest of saving the customer (and you) time and aggravation, I recommend to all users to spend no more than 15 minutes reviewing the application itself for operator error. For example, review any options in the application to determine if there has been a change made that may have been the cause that prompts their question. If the user doesn't see the data expected in an export, review all selection options. If the user is still unable to resolve the issue, spend 15 minutes perusing the User's Guides, KB articles, and FAQ's. If the user is still not able to get an answer, then by all means, invite them to send the email, or pick up the phone. When scheduling a specific time for a phone appointment, be sure to ask the user to include the scheduled time in their zone. All too often, when left up to the user, the time for the zone is incorrectly stated. And that means wasting time rescheduling.

I always extend the professional courtesy of offering support services to my customers who must contract with an outside IT organization to administrate their IT requirements. Scheduling can be a challenge, as you may have appointments scheduled out several days, or even weeks. And the IT consultant is likely in the same boat. I consider a scheduled appointment with a third party the highest priority and must not be canceled. However, one of the most irritating circumstances is when the customer schedules the IT consultant without letting me know. Naturally the customer calls and expects me to drop everything just because their IT guy has just arrived onsite. This shows a total lack of organization and time management on the part of the customer, not to mention the lack of consideration for the position I am in.

There is no real solution to educating this type of customer, especially since they tend to be repeat offenders. When this happens to me, I respond to them as though it was a routine support call, in other words, first come, first serve.

Email vs. Phone

Each method of correspondence has its advantages. Email is extremely useful for short, to-the-point questions or other minor issues. I suggest a maximum of about a paragraph or two with perhaps two to three appropriate (attached or embedded) screen shots describing the inquiry, and keeping to one specific inquiry per email. Upon reviewing the email, the process of resolving the inquiry can begin. Depending on the complexity of the issue or question, follow up may be made by additional email inquires or a phone call. And, I can easily monitor incoming email while I am on the phone.

This works out nicely for me being on the West Coast because East Coast customers can email their inquires on their way out the door for the day. Since that's mid afternoon for me, often times I can have a resolution to their inquiry first thing their next morning. At some point, a question or issue will become too time consuming to convey via email and would be better suited to handle by phone and PC to PC connection session. My interest in addition to providing an answer quickly is expedience and saving time.

If the support inquiry is routine and I feel the user should already know the answer, I will refer the user to a specific area within the User's Guide. I will also describe how I searched the User's Guide using keywords to locate the section containing the answer. I may also refer the user to our website's posted Knowledge Base (KB) articles and FAQ's.

By referring the user to available tools hopefully teaches them to do a little research on their own before compulsively picking up the phone or sending an email. I do explain to the user that these tools are meant to supplement support the Help Desk provides, not replace it. After all, you need to consider the fact they pay for support. And you know the boss wants those checks to keep arriving.

Junk Email

You must always check junk email to make sure legitimate email didn't somehow get tagged as junk. Sort junk email by subject, its quicker and easier to review and delete because there tends to be a lot of junk email with the same subject. Never, ever, unsubscribe, or opt out of junk email unless you know the sender. Opting out of spammed email just makes your email address worth $.001 instead of $.0001 because the spam source now knows you've paid specific attention to it. Besides, it's not likely the opt-out on spam will work. Don't forget to mention your email address when leaving voice messages, and in your phone greetings if appropriate. Always include your email address in the signature area along with your name, company name, address, and phone numbers. Users aren't going to necessarily know all they have to do is click on the sender line to get your email address.

Managing Email

I have seen Inboxes with literally thousands of emails. I can't imagine anybody actually able to mange their email without some kind of filing system. I maintain sub-folders in my email application for each client by company name for all email received from that company.

Since I generally enforce "one-point-of-contact" for corporate customers, sorting by specific users within a company is not necessary. Each group of sub-folders for company names beginning with A through E are saved in a folder called "A thru E", same for those with F thru N, and O thru Z. These sub-folders are saved under a main folder called "Company Name", under the Inbox.

In addition to managing email correspondence from users, I also set up a host of other folders for correspondence from the boss, from other members of the technical staff, and for email received for a specific topic. As soon as I resolve an incoming email, I file it. Thus, my Inbox is my "to-do" list. I'm sure there are many other preferred methods and applications to manage large quantities of email. My method is simple, it doesn't break, and uses an existing application.

Prioritizing

The Help Desk prioritizes support responses based on the severity of the situation. The most severe support request is considered to be the client who cannot resume business due to catastrophic failure of it's' computer systems. The next highest priority is the scheduled telephone appointment. After that, responses are on a first-come, first-serve basis.

Save/File Email, CYB

CYB amounts to nothing more than saving all correspondence, including written, but more importantly, email. The trick is to keep your mailboxes and paper files organized so if you do have to go back to an email a year ago, you can find it. What little I do maintain on paper, are at best thrown into a drawer in approximate chronological order.

CYB is used in extreme cases such as researching the history of a specific problem particularly if the same software problem from a year ago resurfaces. Knowing the history can same a lot of time correcting it if it's already been documented. The alternative is having someone in the programming department sit down and start from scratch.

Keeping all email correspondence allows you to assemble a timeline of responses to specific user issues. This allows management determine any politics that may result when contract support is up for renewal. On many occasions I've caught customers lying about lack of support responses or turnover time for problem resolution. Having the historical email correspondence, even if it's just an acknowledgement of receipt of an email, can mean the difference of losing or keeping a client's business. Most importantly for you, if there are any questions about whether you responded to a user request, if it was in a timely manner, and were you maintaining a professional attitude, nothing better than to CYB with all that email you saved. It's the gift that keeps on giving, and could save your job.

Task Scheduler

I'll be brief on this one. I'm never ceased to be amazed at the amount of Post-It abuse that exists, and how often I see those large desk calendars with so many notes I can't read them. I don't understand why anyone wouldn't take advantage of a Task Scheduler. It's so simple to use. And, you'll never be late. Depending of the type of support event, I will often schedule a time and day to perform installations of updates, basic tutorials, and anytime a support incident involves a third party or IT consultant. Another CYB technique: nobody can tell me I was early or late on a scheduled call so long as I called at the pre-arraigned time.

And, use a time sync application to synchronize your workstation's clock with NORAD, or some other institution with an atomic clock. When someone says you're late (but you're actually right on time), point out the fact that your clock is synced with the atomic clock at NORAD. Case closed.

Chapter 6 Managing the Customer

Condescending

Unless you are dealing with an IQA (Intelligence Quota, Advanced), I have learned being authoritative (and, of course, professional at all times) helps you maintain control. When walking a user through a series of steps designed to troubleshoot a problem, insist on having them proceed with your specific instructions. Don't let them dictate to you how to perform the diagnosis. After all, if they're expert, then why did they call you in the first place? This doesn't justify directing a condescending attitude towards the user on your part though. However, I'm not here to hold tea service, I'm here to conduct business and the user must recognize that fact that not all of your email and phone correspondence are going to be full of candy and flowers.

How long will this take?

I attempt to define the difference between a task and a project. A task might be defined as inserting a bolt in a hole. A project may be defined as completing the insertion of all of the bolts in their holes. I can understand that if one works on an assembly line, there is a finite period of time that inserting a bolt into a hole will take. Multiply that period of time by the number of bolts that need to be inserted into a hole and you have the total amount of time the project will take. You're not working on an assembly line. There is almost always no way to effectively estimate how long a bug will take to correct since you're probably not the programmer, or how long it will take to bring the email server back up, unless you are the network admin.

I like to use the analogy about taking your car in for repair when discussing estimates of "how long will it take" to the user. I ask the user what answer he expects from his mechanic when posed with this question. I ask the user, in our hypothetical situation, if he thinks the mechanic is going to know what the problem is before he can has a chance to get under the hood to perform the diagnoses. Any what happens if "in addition to new brakes, you need the rotors turned and a new master cylinder". The amount of time the repair (and cost) will take has just tripled.

Of course, your user isn't satisfied with your (my) brilliant analogy. So, try quoting my classic IT paradox: "To the layperson, seemingly difficult things can be done easily on a computer; and seemingly simple things are difficult to do on a computer". Changing the size of a fixed length field in a legacy app (which likely will require changes in perhaps thousands of places in the source code) is an ideal example of what a layperson would think might be easy.

Since projects typically include more than one task, then a project is ultimately going to be more time consuming. My general rule for arriving at the total amount of time any task or project will take is to take the "final" estimate, multiply it by two and add forty percent. The point is, the "final" estimate is probably coming from a conglomeration of sales managers, programming, and IT departments. Since you have vast experience as a liaison with all facets of your organization, you know that the programming department hasn't factored in time for QA or development of a conversion program, sales doesn't care except for their commission, and executive management doesn't want to have anything to do with it in the first place. The bottom line is that I would rather listen to the customer complain about an up-front lengthy estimate, than hear them really whine when the task or project is late. And, you're the one that's going to take the flack.

Rarely, will you get a break from having to zero in on some estimated amount of time. My experience with data conversions, as an example, the customer usually understands the complexity of the situation. When asked how long a data conversion takes, my response is "Typically weeks as opposed to days or months, depending on how clean the data is." This statement doesn't pin me down to delivering a production product next week, but it had better be done in less than six months. The morel to this story is, if it is better to give than to receive, expect to give – a lot.

Interacting with Management, Yours and Theirs

I have learned the hard way, more than once, to be extremely careful about your dialog during all phone conversations. While it should go without saying that extreme care must be used on speaker phones, I have actually had the president of the company secretly listening in on my conversation with his employee while attempting to resolve a problem. Anytime there is a dispute, say, over whether specific contractual commitments have been satisfied, it's simply not appropriate for you or the customer on the other end to engage. Rather, you have a boss, and he/she has a boss, this is an issue for the bosses to lock horns.

Liaison with the IT Department

As a former Network Administrator and now Help Desk Tech from the vendor side, I understand the concerns your client's IT department has. I have, for the most part, had the luxury of supporting a reasonably stable system (and, in each case in my career, that's because I worked my butt off to get systems stable).

My technique for easing those concerns their IT department may have is simple: I invite anyone who wishes to attend the initial installation of all applications as a demonstration of how well things DO work. I realize of course, that something always goes wrong during such a session, but it's a risk worth taking. The point you want to emphasize is once things are installed, data converted and delivered, and the users have at least basic training, the only time you'll be calling the IT department with a problem is when they already know they have one!

Missing Person

As a Help Desk Tech in support of an accounting system for publishers, I fielded more than my fair share of good ones. Seems to me, the big crisis are going to happen either right when you enter the door to your office on Monday morning, or right when you get ready to leave on Friday evening.

This one was first thing Monday morning. A user had already sent me a barrage of emails detailing the fact that she had entered a customer into the system, and now it had completely vanished. I let this one go for a couple hours (this is a "technique" I describe in this guide), but then I started getting the phone calls. After several call/hang ups (love those), I finally returned the call. I asked the user what the name of the person was. I asked her to search by Last Name using the missing customer's first name. There it was. She had reversed the entry of the first and last names!

You'll get a lot of ones that fall into the "dah" category, patience is the name of the game. All in fun and strictly within my support and programming departments, I have created a "support call of the month" award, and ceremonially honored the user with the lamest inquiry (in effigy, of course). This was a mock award ceremony for just the techs, a way to boost morel.

Phones, Yes I Have a Few Pointers for Phones Too

Discussing phone etiquette is beating a dead horse, once again it's mostly just common sense. It's always irritating when someone leaves a message after downing a six pack of Red Bull, they speak so fast you have replay the thing ten times just to get their number. The flip side to that one are those that leave the Gettysburg Address, and you know they're going to repeat it when you return their call. Oh, and finally, their phone number at the very end. So when you leave a voice message, do the user a favor. Leave your name, company name, date, day, time (don't forget time zone if applicable), and return number first, then a brief message. Speak clearly, slowly, and enunciate. The same applies for your recorded greetings. I use the same wording for the "I'm on another call" greeting as the "I'm away from my desk" greeting. It is not necessary for customers to know anything other than "I'm on another call". This little tip helps encourage the use of email.

Tip: How many times have you tried to navigate a phone system to get a hold of an IT guy, or somebody else that never picks up and failed? Easy, dial the direct line or extension for their sales department. I guarantee somebody will answer. Then ask for the person you are trying to get hold of.

Seasoned Users

One my professional "weaknesses" (see You the Interviewee) has been to overextend handholding with experienced users. This often sets a precedence making you a virtual walking encyclopedia available for everything anytime. The following is an example of an email dialog I used to help prevent users from taking advantage of my support resources:

"Hi Jim,

We are changing credit card processing companies and would like assistance setting up the new field mappings.

Regards,
Mary

Hi Mary,

I need answers to a few questions before I can proceed:

1. Does your new credit card processing vendor require a text file similar to your old vendor?
2. What fields does the new vendor require and is there a specific order?
3. How does the new vendor handle refunds?

Assuming your new vendor is similar in functionality to the old vendor, the only change necessary is to redefine the field mapping file to support your new vendor. The field mapping file tells what fields are to be exported from ACME Widgets and ultimately imported to your new card processing company.

Defining a field mapping file is described in detail on page 245 of the ACME Widgets User's Guide.

Regards,
Jim"

The initial inquiry from this experienced user is a common, well documented inquiry, and an easy procedure. Note, however, I didn't just blow her off, rather I requested answers to questions necessary for me to assist her with resolving her issue. The fact that I included a brief synopsis and a reference to the User's Guide, and along with the prior questions, it became evident to her this will take less time if she just resolved it on her own. And, of course, I am not discouraging any additional correspondence on the matter should she require further assistance.

Supporting Their Accounting Department

This is an area that must be approached with diplomacy. I dread accountants and controllers primarily because they have virtually no knowledge of issues such as rounding, truncating, and even associative or commutative properties of arithmetic in a digital environment. If their calculator arrives at a number, then by golly, your number better be exactly the same. Most of the problems that arise because a bean counter doesn't like your numbers is because there is no industry standard that dictates exactly how the numbers are to be computed. Or, there may be many industry standards.

In the financial services industry, brokerages and clearing houses have no industry standard for computing share prices. I've seen some of these organizations round at four, five, or even six places, while some truncate at three places. In the publishing industry they have something called earned and deferred income.

These are computed by simply multiplying per issue cost times the number of issues served or number of issues to be served, respectively. And yet, there are those who question this simple calculation. Oh, and they always want to see another report that reconciles with the report they were given. Somebody tell me why you would want to have more than one report in an accounting application that shows the same number? Then try explaining that, even if there was another report, it's still coming from the same data. I review much of this topic in the section on Reports and Reconciliation.

Bottom line, if they're not satisfied with your answer, you're going waste a lot of time explaining why you don't know why.

Take Control, But Listen to the User

Regardless of which end of the phone conversation or email correspondence you are on, customer service and technical support is always an emotional event. To what degree of emotion can be limited by you if you learn to take, and maintain, control of the situation at all times. As soon as you lose control, you've lost any confidence the user may have had in you to resolve their issues. You must keep in mind that the user also has bosses that want the problem solved, and in turn have to keep their customers.

An excellent example are Yackers (I suppose I should have created a special profile for them), especially when there are a bunch of them at the same time on a speaker phone, all yakking at you about 3 dozen things other than the initial inquiry. When this happens to me, I give them a choice: one issue at a time, or adios the speaker phone. Let them know you've got to focus on one issue at a time.

Use Analogies

Using analogies to convey basic concepts quickly is a highly effective technique which most often applies to novice users. One example when explaining file maintenance procedures is to equate the hard drive, folders and files to a physical filing cabinet. I describe to the user that the filing cabinet represents the hard drive, each drawer of the cabinet is like a folder, the manila file folders in a drawer might be a sub-folder, and finally, I compare the paperwork within the manila filing folder to a digital file. I emphasize file maintenance because I discourage storing word processing documents, spreadsheets, and text files within an applications' data folder or installation folder.

Another example I use to describe a shared file, such as a file that stores customer names and addresses, is to think of the shared file as the hub of a wagon wheel. Each spoke of the wagon wheel points outward to other files containing pointers, or "add-on" records.

Weaning the New Customer

One of the more difficult tasks is to get new users to think on their own without upsetting the apple cart. They have had their hand held now for several months via extensive training and one-on-one phone support. I start the process of cutting the umbilical by gradually delaying all responses by phone, and forcing the issue of fielding inquires by email. This technique is a variant of the one I use for entry level inquires from seasoned users whereby I delay responding to either email or voice message to see if they can figure it out on their own. I teach the new user to include screen shots in their email. I respond as much as possible with references to the User's Guide, Knowledge Base (KB) articles, and Frequently Asked Questions (FAQ's) on the web site.

Depending on the "crisis", instead of taking the call immediately, I will email with a request to schedule a day and time to call and connect and address any issues they may have. Establishing and enforcing a one-point-of-contact rule is essential for maintaining control and providing the best possible support. And I explain this to the client.

Note: although you may not have the luxury of selecting when you want to take calls, I have found more than half of all calls which go to voice mail are just call hang-ups. My rule for voice messages is: if they don't leave a message, then it must not have been important. And, I'm delighted they didn't waste my time on something trivial.

Software Development companies who provide applications to a niche industry virtually always have some type of arrangement for technical support beyond point-of-sale. Most applications I have supported are sold with six months or one year subscription support at no charge. Beware of the new clients who will pound you everyday for support, will expect you to do as much of their work as possible, and squeeze whatever resources they can get – before their free term for subscription support expires. Why? Because they have no intention of spending anything beyond the original sale. I have only recently learned to foresee this event. And when I do suspect this is the case, I don't give in to unreasonable support requests, I stick to the rules regardless of the amount of pressure. You can try to explain this one to your boss, but I doubt it will do any good. But CYA just in case you're wrong on your read.

Chapter 7 User Profiles: Who, What, and How

I have no intention of offending anyone, but if you see your profile in this chapter, then simply put: sometimes the truth hurts. So before I go into more support strategies, techniques, and management, I thought I could take a break by introducing you to a lighter look at part of the cross section of society you should expect to have to correspond with.

No doubt you will be dealing with a wide spectrum of all levels of users. Here I have defined a number of profiles I think best illustrates the types of people you will be interacting with. I firmly believe that networking with people who have "problems", and even those that don't, on a daily basis is the most challenging task of the Help Desk Technician. The best approach is to keep all correspondence with users at a professional level. I have made the mistake a few times of getting too personal. I've actually had gals and *guys* literally break down on me during a support session. It wasn't because I was mean, and I'm not a collections agent or anything. But this behavior illustrates the level of stress which exists, especially for those who may not be adequately competent for the position they're expected to perform.

While building a personal relationship with a user can work (it depends on how "personal"), it can turn into something like having your ex-wife as a co-worker. So, be careful on that one.

"ID" Ten "T"

ID10T's want you to do their job for them. ID10T's never inform you the problem has been resolved when you do get back to them. Naturally, that always results in "Well, as long as I have you….", followed with ten other things they want YOU to do for them. One technique I have found effective, is to respond to issues by referring users back to the User's Guide (aka RTFM, acronym for READ THE EFFING MANUAL). Even better, keep referring them to your Knowledge Base and FAQ sections on your website.

Caffeine Junkies

Whether it's natural metabolism, or powered by high caffeine and sugar "energy" drinks, people who don't let you finish your sentence before cutting in with yet another question, are among the worst I've had to deal with. I have to use my "Take Control" approach on these user types. My best advice to a chronic buttinski is cut in on the question they cut you off with, and ask them if you can please finish answering the initial question before moving on (I have to take breath now). This type of user is the most likely to leave a phone message which sounds like the statement of liabilities at the end of some prescription drug radio ad. At the end of the message, the phone number is spoken so quickly you can't quite get all of it the first go. Now you have to listen to the entire message again and hopefully get the phone number in its entirety.

Here's another one, and it usually happens as soon as I get into the office for the day. While going through my voice mail, a user has left a series of "crisis" messages to call back immediately. During the time I am going through the voice messages, he's already left three or four more.

As I proceed to listen to the next batch, he leaves yet ANOTHER three or four more. Seriously folks, this stuff happens. I couldn't make this stuff up.

Chicken Little Syndrome

The CLS profile includes new users and users who are especially terrified of change. The slightest occurrence of events outside of what they have defined as their universe will cause them to hit the panic button. Assuming you are supporting an application mission critical to your customers, bank on the fact you are going to get a call for every problem. This includes network issues, problems with other applications that have nothing to do with you, questions about regulatory issues, hangnails, you name it.

CLS users need to be assured, with the exception of intentional maliciousness, they cannot break the system. Establishing as high a level of confidence in the systems you support as possible will improve the situation. CLS users are prone to a high rate of data entry errors such as switching first and last names (now they can't find the record they've just entered), or wondering why the system won't accept L7J 0A1 as the zip code for Ontario, California.

CLS'ers tend to blame everything on you and your application. This is particularly true of users who experience problems due to an ongoing unstable platform. Cries of "wrong options were mysteriously selected" are commonplace. The CLS user will never fault themselves, especially if the mistake causes significant loss of time and money. I suggest implementing "CYB" (see Cover Your Backside). You may need to prove that someone is actually lying.

Clueless

The "I have no clue" types are oblivious to all things even remotely technical. They are quite comfortable with having their IT guy show up every morning to free 20mb Yes, that's megabytes) of hard drive space so they can be up and running for the day (believe it or not, this is a true story). How do I know this? Because I got the call the first time they ran out of disk space and wondered why nothing worked. Their reasoning of course, was because the IT guy didn't show up that day. In an extreme case such as this, all you can do is suggest a hardware upgrade or approach the problem from a file maintenance aspect. It's likely you won't be hearing much from these users. Another good example, and true story, that fits this category are those who "don't want to upgrade because I'm going to retire in five years and I don't want to touch a thing".

On one occasion the user sent me a CD via overnight carrier. It was the only way I could get their data since they were unable to hit my FTP, and I couldn't access theirs. Anyway, when I asked for the tracking number, the response was "I'll be dropping it off at a box, I don't think I'll get any tracking info. If I do you'll be the first to know." Hmmm.

Completely Helpless

Another classic profile. You'll wonder who zips up their pants in the morning. You'll also start wondering very soon if this one is ever going to get it. Cranium to brain ratio is equivalent to a bb in a boxcar. An excellent example is the employee that has been there for twenty years – before the office was "automated". This person has never even considered training in basic computer skills. They have been managing the office on paper ledger for over two decades.

Now, it's time for them to upgrade. An excellent definition of "impossible" is: dribbling a football. Another one is trying to teach Completely Helpless how to use a mouse verbally over the phone. I don't envy you.

Note: I have often wondered, we're the wealthiest, most powerful country in the world. How in the hell do these people survive? And, they're probably making twice as much as I am.

Could Have Been the World's Greatest Spy

Ever notice that when you attempt to get an answer to a simple Yes or No question from some folks, that you get a reading of the Call of Wild before the actual "Yes" or "No"? This one was a late afternoon panic call. Many accounting applications, including the one I supported at the time, require a month-end close. That also means that no users other than the administrator can be logged into the application during the time of close. And, if anything goes south during the close, you have to restore from backup and start all over. This user could have been one of the world's great spies. He reported the close had failed, and there was "computer language" all over his screen. I spent a solid thirty minutes asking about what changes on the network there could have been, was there anybody else logged in, power outage, disk full, etc. Finally, *he* asked *me* if the technician hot-swapping a hard drive on the server during the close could have had anything to do with the application failure. Another one for the book.

Emotionally Tanked

There is a very fine line between a personal and professional relationship and great care must be used to stay on top of this one. Unlike office relationships, customers are your bread and butter.

And, they are the bread and butter of the person that signs your paycheck. Pack your stuff in a box and hand in your resignation if you lose a client because you got too personal.

I have had on several occasions, the user break down into tears (both ladies *and* gents). Although I have never pursued a personal relationship in a professional environment, and I don't plan to, I did make the mistake of letting "Emotionally Tanked" get too personal with me. Stuff like "how's the weather out your way?", or "what are you planning for the holiday?" is not out of line. I would encourage such dialog because it strengthens the relationship between client and vendor. When problems arise, levels of frustration remain minimal because the client has confidence in you, and you appreciate their patience.

I can't define "too personal" for you. You'll have to rely on common sense. When (not if) things appear to get too personal, get past the personal stuff quickly, get to the business at hand. I would say something like "excuse me, may I put you on hold for a moment", then do so. Give them a minute or so, get back on, and inform them that your boss needs to see you immediately following this service call. If the calls start coming, respond with email letting the offending user know you're busy and to please email the inquiry. Anything incriminating in the email will obviously be on record, and hopefully this situation stands down.

Empire Builder

You know this type just from your experience with new co-workers.

New employees want to establish themselves as soon as possible (not that I discourage this, in fact it's necessary for survival), but there must be a line drawn where use of diplomacy and common sense should be observed. New co-workers can be readily dealt with if they get too aggressive because they reside under your corporate auspices. All you have to do is complain to your HR department.

But what do you do about the new user just hired by one of your best clients? You're in Tech Support and you have to deal with them just like you have to deal with everyone else. This new user is going to be aggressive, demanding, and impatient. But, I have a few suggestions.

EB's have a tendency to run bawling immediately to their boss if they don't get immediate gratification. I had one experience with a new user (a complete novice) who absolutely insisted that I fix her slow workstation. I attempted to explain that performance issues were not something I could assist with and that her concerns should be directed to her IT department. Her response was simply "I don't care how it gets fixed, I want it fixed." I didn't respond to that email, as far as I was concerned my obligation for this support inquiry had already ended. Evidently, she then complained to her boss because a day later I received a call from one of her IT staff. He had found some issues with their antivirus application that was set to perform scans on every file the relational database engine was opening. He agreed to inform her of the resolution of her performance issues. The point here was to basically put her in her place. Get her to realize these types of issues are not going to be resolved by waving the magic wand I happen to have in my back pocket at the moment her majesty decides she needs action on some perceived problem.

A similar incident occurred when a newbie had been trying to compose invoice documents that worked in conjunction with the application I supported at the time. She sent me en email requesting a template file that was documented in the User's Guide, but could not be found on her workstation. I sent the correct file knowing she probably already had it. But, since the filename of the file I sent her didn't match that which she had seen in the User's Guide, she went right to the boss: "He didn't send me the correct file". And I promptly received an email from the boss asking about the file. I did a little research and found that she had been reading a User's Guide that was ten years old (one would think to look at revision dates in manuals and guides?). I responded to her boss' email letting him know that I found the reference to the file they were looking for in a ten year old manual. I recommended he download the latest version of the User's Guide (which they already had in octuplicate but I didn't want to rub it in), and let him know I would be delighted to confirm they also had the latest version of the application to match the current Guide. I suggested to her boss that it would be helpful in the future to emphasize to his staff the importance of being more observant and providing enough information for me to continue to provide excellent support. In this case, a screen shot of the page would have saved considerable time and aggravation for all involved, and would have avoided unnecessarily concerning the big boss, especially on such a trivial matter.

Oh, and I cc'd his staff with that reply, and never had any more EB issues with that user.

Excessive Compulsive

Maximize email and limit phone correspondence as much as possible with EC's. Like others, EC not only wants you to do all of their work, but also correspond with their company CEO, Controller, and IT department.

There is usually an inordinate amount of unnecessary attention paid to detail. One situation that comes to mind was one of my distributors that complained about an invoice that was off by a nickel, yes, $.05 out of tens of thousands of dollars. And I had to figure it out. Turns out, they were calculating sales tax incorrectly. I spent half a day debugging someone else's system. One of my common sense definitions applies to EC's, and that is to never trust a spreadsheet from them or anyone else.

I Don't Have Anything To Do!

Another type that mostly applies to you guys and gals that serve in-house staff, IDHATD's are right up there with the TS'ers. This has got to be one of the top five stupidest things to say out loud. I once witnessed an employee clear off her desk, sit back, fold her hands, and exclaim to the entire front office that she had NOTHING to do. And she was going to relax the rest of the afternoon. The next day, she had something to do – pack her stuff and permanently exit out the office door.

I once had the unfortunate task of discreetly logging productivity for a specific individual in the repair lab. This was where technicians would repair equipment returned by our customers. This guy was the senior technician, and he was under scrutiny for not pulling his own weight. He had been caught for too many breaks, taking lunch without clocking out, then clocking out later for "lunch", and a host of other offenses. I had warned him many times over that year he ought to get his gig together. I dropped by the lab one day, his work area was spotless, he was just standing there with his arms folded doing absolutely nothing. Meanwhile, the backlog of repairs continued to grow. I told him, "Mark, as long as you're going to stand there and do nothing, at least pull a station apart and scatter some tools on your bench so it looks like you're doing something!".

He didn't listen. He was gone the following week. And to this day he blames me for getting fired.

I have a "Quick Question"

This depends on whose definition of "quick". Be prepared to pull a refill of whatever you drink and settle in for these. There is no such thing as a quick question. And more often than not, the initial question leads into a host of a bazillion other questions. And, QQ seems to have a quick question about every other day. This is more obnoxious than listening to loose quarters in the dryer. If your organization defines a line between support and training (see the chapter on Technical Support, Training, and Maintenance), then perhaps this user needs additional formal (paid) training.

Immediate Gratification (see also "How Long Will This Take", and "Empire Builders")

This profile tips you off pretty quickly. During the process of establishing an Internet connection to address a given support issue, IG's are going to constantly inquire as to whether or not you are connected. I explain (each and every time) that the connection process is going to take a few minutes because there is always latency in my network, their network, or somewhere in between. I let them know when the connection has been authenticated at each stage, and when I finally acquire full keyboard and mouse access to their workstation. It never ceases to amaze me that those who seek immediate gratification seem to be the most likely procrastinators.

Intelligence Quota: Advanced

Working with advanced users can be just as, or even more challenging than those with no experience.

Advanced users with a lot of paper (degrees and certificates plastered all over their walls, and they let you know about it) and little real world experience are often aggressive, arrogant, and "know more than you". I have found it very rare to work with someone with a balance of knowledge, common sense, and attitude. When this happens, make a note of this person. Always attempt to secure this individual for all future events. Even rarer, is stumbling upon someone who is actually *sharper* than you! Advice for this situation is simple: keep your mouth shut, eyes and ears open, and learn something. I have noticed that IQA's tend to have excellent memories. They can recall events in the past, and I'm talking years, that often play a significant role in solving the problem at hand.

Intelligence Quota: Room Temperature

If there is such a thing as "average", then this cross-section of the general population is perhaps the least difficult to contend with. There are few extremes with these personalities. Most things are taken in stride and there is an overall understanding that things will get fixed and life will continue to move on. It's too bad that "average" seems to be such a minute minority.

Intelligence Quota: Uh, You Got Problems

On a scale of one to ten, one being the worst, these folks are a one and a half at best. Yet somehow they were able to get to a position requiring some responsibility, a few analytical skills, and a little common sense.. I consider myself an expert with the ability to correspond with all levels of users with the ultimate objective of resolving their issues, present concepts which can be grasped, and enhance productivity. Unfortunately, this is a finite assertion on my part.

On occasion during a support session I'll notice unusually long pauses in conversation after I have made a statement about a support or training issue. I have no choice but to ask the question: "Pardon me, are you waiting for me, or am I waiting for you?". Of all of the profiles, this is the most exhaustive.

Know-It-All

This type insists on dominating the conversation and telling you how to perform your job, etc. Putting it simply: "if you know the answer, then why are you calling me?". Never ask a KIA "How do you know the refrigerator light turns off when you shut the door?", or you'll likely get engaged in some convoluted debate about the subject. The necessary tactic for dealing KIA's is ignore their dribble, get the problem resolved, and move on. In extreme cases, you may have to cut in on whatever they're babbling about for questions, or hopefully, to inform them you're done. Always agree with whatever questions or philosophies a "Know-It-All" my throw at you. Hmmm, this applies to bosses as well now that I think about it.

Beware, Know-It-All's will download an update via FTP to each and every workstation separately instead of downloading it once, then pulling it down to each workstation from a network drive.

Knows Just Enough to be Dangerous

This profile is just more aggravating then anything else. These folks tend to be middle to upper management with little or no technical background, and more often than not, they admit to it!. They're IT wannabes. They tend to micromanage. I seek resolution to their inquiry as quickly as possible because they cost you a lot of time.

You will end up repeating most everything to him even though his staff person completely understands. He will have many, many questions. Worst of all, unless you avoid him, you will be spending an abundant amount of time fixing all of the stuff that he breaks.

Bosses at the customer end are generally the least desirable people to deal with regarding day to day operations. That's why he has hired staff. This is one situation that justifies your bosses' existence. Your boss must correspond with their boss and suggest (insist) the point of contact be someone other than him. He can be showered with such phrases as "Dave can work it out with Mary, and then Mary can follow up with you via an email".

Misery Loves Company

I've always believed the old saying "never say never", but you can never make these folks happy. Not even in a perfect world. MLC's always make sure that you know how frustrated they are and what a pain in the backside everything always is in every email, voice message, and of course, any conversation. They take every opportunity to induce jabs at how inefficient, poorly designed, and difficult to use your application is. My position on handling MLC's is to be firm in letting them know that you are not the complaint department, and to please include only pertinent facts on issues they are inquiring about. This behavior is a waste of time having to read through correspondence containing all of their personal grievances, is non-productive, and it does nothing for morel.

As much as I hate to say it, there are customers that your company is better off without. Don't ever state this to the boss, though. They don't believe in this theory, they only believe in the bottom line, dollars of course.

I'm reminded of an event in 2007 when a major player in the wireless phone industry "fired" about a thousand of their customers because of the considerable amount of support resources spent on this core group of users. As much as I despise this particular large corporation, I had to applaud their move. I was surprised at the reaction of the industry with this move. Why not dish off the problem accounts to your competitor? Makes sense to me.

Moron Factor, Helping with Hardware

Back in the days when laptops were too expensive, our regional sales managers each had their own desktop computer provided by the company. And of course, one of my tasks was to support those machines. On one occasion, one of the rep's machines' hard drive failed. I told the rep that I didn't need the keyboard, mouse, or any of the cables, just the "box". You guessed it, he sent me an empty box, the one the computer was originally shipped in. Morel to this story, be careful getting too technical with some folks.

Mr. Gadget

When are folks going to realize that you can't drop a Chevy engine into a Ford chassis without suffering the consequences? Dual boot systems such as the Mac that allegedly run "100%" Windows XP, are not 100% compatible. And if you somehow do get your applications to run in this type of rubber band and paper clip operating environment, you're going to have to support it, and it won't take long before it becomes an upper-management level nightmare if things do go south.

Mr. Gadget loves the Swiss Army Knife of software apps, the ones that can do everything. Mr. Gadget is especially fond of shareware and will spend unbelievable amounts of time making Windows 98 workstations work with the latest versions of anything. Mr. Gadget tends to have about twenty applications open at the same time, all of the time. He has no less than three different antivirus applications and software firewalls deployed simultaneously. He's constantly calling you wanting to know why his system is so slow.

Cheap Mr. Gadgets are willing to take things even further. One of my favorites is what was known as "Sneaker Net" years ago before networks became reliable and cost effective. Sneaker net is nothing more than a bunch of non-networked workstations, one of which is known as "live" (paint a cup red, and whoever has the red cup is "live"). From the live workstation, someone runs around copying the production data to the other workstations presumably for "read-only" operations. Hence the term.

Even today, I get inquires from users who want to work at home but not have to connect to the corporate LAN. This means current production data is copied from the original location on a corporate LAN to a remote PC. The user works at home over the weekend and updates the LAN on Monday morning. All too often, users lose track of which database is "live" and end up copying an old version of data over the current production data. I've seen weeks of lost data entry from just one instance where someone lost track of who had what and when. Never recommend Sneaker Net.

Mr. Gadget will pull a decommissioned workstation out of the back closet, install a server OS on the old workstation (because he's too cheap to buy a server), all under the semblance of saving a few bucks and insisting on how clever he is. He gets it up and running, and for the next month wonders why his applications moved from a workgroup configuration to a client-server environment are constantly crashing, losing data, and corrupting files. Dozens, maybe hundreds, of man-hours are spent restoring backups, attempting to repair corrupted files, and troubleshooting cause. This scenario actually played out for me one time. Finally, one of the IT guys inserted a thumb drive into the "server" and it died instantly. Just to confirm, he did it a couple more times with the same result. When I found out about it, I gave them two options: put the network back to the original peer-to-peer, or purchase a real server. Otherwise, I was not going to continue supporting their current hardware configuration. They opted for the latter, and never had any of the same problems again.

Office Politics

From time to time you may happen upon a user with a severe case of "Office Politics". This is where users within the same organization you correspond with don't get along and they play you against each other much like small children will try to play mom against dad. One simple solution to avoid this situation is by enforcing the one point of contact rule. When I sense a situation where office politics is affecting me by easting my tine, I get blunt and ask who is having problems with whom. Beyond that, I state the nature of my job as that of a Help Desk Technician and I will not be party to their personnel problems. Unless, of course, they are willing to pay my hourly fee of $300.00 for psychiatric consultation.

Phobias, Computerphobia?

I've had a little fun with these types. Walking a user through a series of keystrokes and mouse clicks to jump start a task is common. I would pick my prey and when asked if it was OK to click Delete, I would say yes. Immediately upon their clicking OK, I would exclaim "Oh, gees, no, wait!". That gets 'em every time!

Seriously, computerphobic users are difficult to work with. They will question everything you do. They do not want to jeopardize the day's work and rightly so. Computerphobic users will not try anything new for fear they will either destroy data or break their computer.

I learned a way to approach this user category from my brother, a practicing dentist for nearly a quarter century. As he performed various dentist things on me, he would continue a dialog by informing me of everything he was either about to, or in the process of doing. From the initial examination, to x-rays, shots, drilling, and filling, he told me whether it would hurt or not, and otherwise what to expect.

When I am performing troubleshooting with a user, especially a computerphobic user, I essentially narrate what I am doing. I periodically ask if it is OK to copy a file, create a backup, or restart the workstation. Since you are dealing with a computerphobic user, by definition, the call originated as a result of a situation that has elevated into a "crisis". I have found that using this narrative technique quells a lot of the anxiety, instills confidence in your abilities to resolve issues, and induces a warm, fuzzy feeling on the part of the user. Note that this technique is not limited to use on computerphobes only.

Sugar Daddy's

Sugar Daddy's are my way of describing a situation where a spouse is put in control of some part (or all) of company operations by way of nepotism. This is entirely acceptable, except when the spouse given control is incompetent and otherwise unqualified for the position. The spouse given control is usually insecure and yet has some clue he or she lacks the necessary skills (by a long shot) for the position. As a result, he or she is has the Napoleon complex, and you can tell just by interacting with his or her employees. The employees are reluctant to accept any responsibility for fear of repercussion. It's the classic "walking on egg shells" environment. How does this impact you? You're going to be expected to spend dozens, perhaps hundreds of hours over the course of the next few months teaching the basics to someone who hasn't a clue. Making things worse, remember Sugar Daddy? He or she is in total denial, and is going to adamantly protect the inept spouse at all cost. This is a circumstance whereby you must enforce your support contract (see Appendix F) to the fullest extent. If things really get ugly, let the bosses lock horns. That's what they get paid for.

The Tammy Syndrome and Team Work

Tammy Syndrome applies generally to those of you who run a Help Desk for in-house staff. The symptoms of Tammy Syndrome are employees that only fulfill their original job description. They refuse to deviate from their daily routine, change is not an option, and they tend to blow you off should you ever offer any suggestions. People afflicted with Tammy Syndrome are the type of staff that never contributes to the team effort. TS'ers live and work within the confines of Tammyland where all is well all of the time. Yet, they constantly complain about not getting any raises or promotions.

Addendum to Tammy Syndrome

I had on experience in particular with an customer service representative affected with severe Tammy Syndrome. She kept downloading back ground images for her desktop, even after being told not to (They wouldn't let me block her Internet access from any of this, go figure). Needless to say, her workstation was the only one which locked up consistently, almost daily. I instructed her to call me when it happened so I could have a chance at resolving the problem. One day while I was in the phone room at the opposite end of the building property (a quarter mile away or so), she called me to come to her desk as her workstation had once again frozen. I dropped what I was doing, and by the time I arrived at her desk she had already restarted her workstation. Thanks a lot.

Whiners

In my opinion, whiners are the most challenging of all the profiles. Whiners not only complain about everything in the most obnoxious mannerisms, they constantly repeat how serious the problem is, how the problem affects their customers and their customers' customers, and so on. Whiners will take advantage of every opportunity to lecture you on topics you are already aware of. Every correspondence, whether voice message, email, or fax, whiners will make sure to remind you of the all of the ramifications of the crisis they are having, over, and over, and over again. If there is one profile I have described, whiners are the ones that will ultimately land me in a rubber room dressed in a straight jacket.

Summary, User Profiles

In summary, and I hate to bring it up, depending on the frequency, severity, and specific types of problems traveling through your department, one might consider maintaining logs on every support issue received. Email should be enough, however, consider logging phone conversations and maintaining progress reports for problem clients. Particularly for conversions and larger custom software development projects.

I've experienced many times where rapport with what I considered an excellent client goes south after many years of a great business relationship. All it takes is a couple of significant events, even those out of your control, to devastate that professional bond. Although my profiles may be a bit of an exaggeration, they are a serious attempt to illustrate the types of people you will be dealing with, and I've had many show their darker sides by lying to cover up mistakes they made by blaming them on me or my staff. I've experienced blatant accusations of maliciously changing data, purposely introducing bugs in software, and even changing network configurations. Appendix F is a working example of a support agreement which offers protection from this type of behavior. If you don't already have this infrastructure in place, I suggest you deploy it immediately.

Too bad really, I remember the days when a client would call me and ask how much a certain software enhancement would cost to implement. I would quote him, he would say "okay". I would deliver the requested enhancement, I would get the check in the mail. All on a verbal "hand shake" over the phone. Gone are those days.

Chapter 8 Inquiring Users Want to Know

These are a few "out of the blue" inquires from users that you might get from time to time. The user always wants to know the cause of a specific problem, even if they're not close to having the skill level or technical knowledge to comprehend cause in most cases. My standard rule is simply to not offer information. When asked a question which can only be answered in technical terms, explain as best you can in layman's terms, use analogies if possible, in other words a bit of a "snow-job" if you have to, and move on.

Data Security, Especially Personal Data

Securing systems to protect against identity theft is a number one priority for all customers who store credit card and other sensitive information. Regulatory agencies are enforcing security requirements by attempting to scan corporate networks and other systems to ensure compliance. Although you are likely not an attorney, or an authorized representative of one of these regulatory agencies, you will receive inquires from your customers for advice. So, I have included this special article which briefly discusses the difference between *encryption* and *masking*, and several of the major issues regarding security compliance with credit card information. It should help make this topic easier to convey these basic concepts to your users:

"Encryption is deployed on the files by software applications that actually store sensitive data such as credit card numbers.

Encryption is transparent to all users because the encrypted credit card numbers are buried deep within these files. Encryption is designed to prevent unauthorized access to credit card numbers in the event these files fall into the wrong hands. Masking is simply a switch in the application that allows the user to control the displaying and printing of either all the digits of credit card numbers, or as masked where only the last four digits appear.

In addition to encryption, most legacy systems store credit card number data in an 'unformatted', or binary format, so only that particular application can read the files it creates and maintains. Once the binary data containing encrypted credit card numbers is read by that application, the credit cards numbers must be unencrypted before they can be used, thus offering a double layer of security. Data encryption helps meet current industry standard compliance with regulatory agencies such as Payment Card Industry (PCI) Security Standards Council. However, since credit card information can and must be available in a readable format for payment processing, the user is responsible for the administration of such files that reside outside of any application that maintains such data. Standards for compliance for data security, including destruction of any printed material containing credit card information, deletion of any digital files containing non-encrypted credit card information, and all devices pertaining to the security of the network are solely the responsibility of the user. Common sense must be adhered to: never email credit card information, not even half of a credit card number in one email, and the other half in another email (duh). Never use a cell phone to communicate credit card or other personal information.

The user must be responsible for setting up and maintaining security on the network (servers and workstations).

Operating systems provide the means to assign usernames, passwords, and levels of authority, also referred to as "credentials", required for users to gain access to specific areas of a network. In the event the network (server and/or workstation) is compromised by an electronic intruder, or by other physical means, the intruder would have to know the credentials of an authorized user to gain access to the network, and would have to know how to use the application in order to obtain credit card information. In addition, many applications offer username and password protection at the user level managed within the application itself. An intruder would also have to know the embedded security within the application thus offering yet another layer of security beyond that of the network."

If you intend to publish guidelines concerning data security such as what I have discussed here, I recommend also including a disclaimer protecting you from any liability. Here is an example:

"Note: This section is not intended to offer legal information or advice. Interested parties are encouraged to consult an attorney, IT professional, and appropriate representatives from any pertinent governing agency regarding the content of this article. The author shall not be liable for any content within this guide."

Details, Details

Occasionally, you'll get a wing nut question like "Why is the page number on the top of your accounting reports?" (I presume as opposed to the bottom of the page). For these and other time wasting and otherwise worthless questions, I offer an explanation behind the history of your company, and the development of the applications you support, using a generic "one-answer-fits-all" that goes something like this:

"XYZ Accounting Software, Inc. has been in business developing commercial applications for the financial services community for over 20 years. In fact, XYZ Accounting Software Inc. began way back in the old DOS days. Our products have evolved through many generations of operating systems, product enhancements, program corrections, programming and management staff. In short, a lot of cooks have stirred the soup. Report formats, data entry methods, field labels, everything you see, for all intents and purposes, is by design. I simply cannot provide an accurate answer to an inquiry of this level of detail other than to say, 'it is by design'".

Then I complete the response with: "We do, however, continue to strive towards greater consistency with regards to report formats, terminology, and compatibility to current technologies through implementation of future releases of our products."

History – Mac vs. PC

I once knew someone whose brother stood next to a Mac. That is the sum total of all my experience and knowledge about Macs except for a little history. It's a sure bet if you're a Windows shop, you're going to field the question "why don't your applications run on a Mac?" on more than a few occasions. My response is the following:

"As a product development manger back in mid 1980's, I was ultimately responsible for making the decision on porting our flagship applications to new environments. Making the decision not to port to Mac was ridiculously simple – the Mac folks wanted upwards of $250,000 for the PRIVELIGE of purchasing their SDK (Software Development Kit, without which, you aren't going to run anything on a Mac).

Not to mention the cost of educating staff on the new platform, operating systems, and development tools, and the man hours to implement the port itself. Meanwhile, DOS was, for all intents and purposes, free. And, the price point for SDK tools for DOS was about the same as those for today's Windows. I believe the excessive cost for the Mac SDK is solely responsible for the five to ten percentile market share the Mac possesses today. I made a similar decision about OS2, only for a different reason. I didn't think it would evolve into a major player within the industry."

Shutdown, or not to Shutdown?

I'd say the jury is still out on this one, even after more than 25 years of debate. I will say this: I had two identical machines, both the same make, model, and even the serial numbers were close. One was for a programmer who shut his down every night. The other was mine, and since I needed the ability to access it after hours, I left mine on all of the time. Curious after 5 years, the only hardware problem was a "bad batch" capacitor issue on the mother board that the manufacturer acknowledged, and repaired under warranty. This happened to both machines a month apart when they were both about 4 years old. I don't think I matters whether you shut it down, or not. I leave mine on because I want the option of being able to remotely access it.

Chapter 9 Education on Arrogance, and More Tech Tips

I'll never forget my very first field service call. The client was the owner of a very well-to-do money management firm in Brentwood, California. The call came first thing in the morning. The client was not able to turn on the computer and demanded that someone be sent to their office immediately to fix the problem. They adamantly refused to perform any troubleshooting over the phone. Anyway, I arrived at the office, took about 30 seconds to analyze the situation. The power cord from the computer was unplugged! Apparently the cleaning staff had run over the cord with a vacuum cleaner. I have since had similar experiences with network cables, phone lines, and printer cables. Morel to this story, as obvious as it is, is to first check that all cords and cables are properly secured when you experience a problem that could be related.

Oh, and on my way out from that call, they asked me to look at their modem. They told me that sometimes it worked, other times it didn't (also known as "intermittent" by anyone with at least a high school education). I found the modem cable had not been secured, so I produced a screwdriver and tighten down the cable. I'm not sure what happened or why, but I offered my screwdriver for them to keep and they went ballistic. As though that was totally beneath them to so much as touch a simple hand tool. I also got the royal chewing out by my boss when I got back. They had immediately called him to report my gross misbehavior. Morel to this story - don't bother to offer wealthy wing nuts any assistance, or a screwdriver, that actually makes sense.

Another form of Thrashing

Cloud Services that provide offsite backups, may fail to achieve the intended goal of consistently backing up files which have changed since the last backup. This happens if you are attempting to backup very large files, such as email stores, which take longer than the time allotted to perform the backup. Email stores are an excellent example for this discussion, not only due to size, but also because they are dynamic. Unless you have extremely fast Internet access, such as T1 or T3, files in the tens of gigabyte range may ultimately take days or even a week to push over the Internet. In this scenario, the Cloud service never actually completes a full backup of this file thus causing it to continually make the attempt and in doing so, ultimately never backs up all of the other files that have changed.

Application Hang

Unless additional details can be provided (for example, screen shots of error messages or informative messages), it is recommended that you restart your server and workstations.

How often do you restart your server(s)? Restarting Windows-based servers at least once a month, whether it appears necessary or not, is a widely accepted industry standard. The Windows operating system is not known for its exemplary housekeeping abilities (allowing buildup of residual processes, maintaining locked records and files unnecessarily, and other anomalies which cause problems of this nature).

When did the symptoms first start occurring? Establishing a timeline can help locate potential problems while reviewing Event Viewers and other network related log files on servers and workstations as error logs are date and time stamped. Packet Collisions, Broadcast Storms, even multiple users streaming Internet can cause serious performance problems on a network. IT department personnel should monitor these issues as a matter of procedure or preventative maintenance.

What has changed on the network? Examples might be new software installations and/or software upgrades. Have there been any new hardware installations or hardware upgrades? Have there been any problems with power in the building? Any one, or a combination, of these items can contribute to network latency issues.

Bad Spot

Hard Drives have moving parts, and they move pretty fast. I'm not going to get into the physics on how it all works, but just like cars, they do wear out. Occasionally, you might run across problems with applications that are failing because the files are read only. Or, you get an error when simply trying to compress a file. Assuming things like access rights have been confirmed to be correct, I recommend making a "rubber stamp" copy of the folder containing the file(s) in question. Rename the original folder with the extension "bad", then rename the copy back to its' original file name. If the problem goes away, then I suspect a physical problem with a specific location on the hard drive. By renaming the folder in question rather than deleting it precludes it from being freed up whereby the OS can write to it again. I see this as a temporary solution, and nothing more than another "process by elimination" tip to locate the cause of the original problem. The real solution is to replace the hard drive.

Connectivity Issues

I once fielded a call from a member of an IT department regarding a "serious problem" with the application that I supported at the time. The problem: he described how the application was up and running fine in one building, but not the other. Hmmm. Could it be, I asked, a networking issue? "No", he replied. "The network's not having any problems". I asked if there was a switch or router in between the server and each of the two buildings. He said yes, so I suggested taking each of the two cables, one for each building, and simply switching the location on the switch where they were physically plugged in. After a few moments, he refused to comply with my suggestion saying that these were fiber-optic cables (Huh?). I have no idea why he made any reference to fiber optic, but I insisted he try what I suggested. I received an email a couple hours later from my user saying all was well! How he ever ended up in an IT department is beyond my comprehension.

There are several common problems that can prevent a user from accessing databases on a network from a workstation. Many applications are designed to "remember" the location of their databases by writing the paths to an "ini" file usually location in the applications' installation folder. This feature precludes the user from continually having to browse for a particular app's data. The user will get an error and will be unable to access an applications' data if that path is located on a disconnected network hard drive. If the user inadvertently redirects an app to a path that does not contain its' own data, or if the application data has changed locations, the app will have to be redirected to that new location. An easy test is to have the user browse the available drives on his workstation and click on the network drive where the application data is stored.

If he gets a "Disconnected Network Drive" error, have him contact his network administrator. If he is able to view the contents of the network drive, then he should be able to launch the application without error.

General Protection Fault, Son of Blue Screen of Death

Occasionally, you may experience a General Protection Fault while in a Windows program. Anytime you experience a General Protection Fault it is an indication that the OS has been interrupted by a set of circumstances that had not previously been accounted for. Since there are perhaps millions of separate software applications in existence, of which there is virtually an unlimited number of combinations of these applications (not to mention dll's, controllers, and drivers) that may cause this problem, there is basically no practical way of determining cause. The immediate solution is simple: restart workstation(s) and server(s).

Occasionally a conflict may exist with DLL's (Dynamically Linked Libraries) between Windows based software applications. If you are experiencing frequent occurrences of General Protection Faults in a particular application, you may want to set the option to "Run in separate memory space" in the properties of the shortcut icon. You can also try running the application as an administrator but you will need administrative credentials to do so. Try installing either one of the applications and see if you continue to get the errors while running the other.

Hot-Swappable Hard Drives

One shop I worked at have a large hard drive array called the "Vault". There were perhaps eight drives, with one side of four drives configured to mirror the other side. Without backing up first, my supervisor proceeded to "hot-swap" one of drives. Guess what? We lost all of the data in the array. And no backup. In my opinion, hot-swappable hard drives are not. It's not worth the time savings of not powering down the machine before swapping out a hard drive, a redundant power supply, or redundant NIC. I also discourage configuring partitions or raid arrays that include more than one physical drive. If you lose one drive, you lose all of them. This is similar to incremental backups which I discuss in another chapter.

Okay, Which File Is It?

The only time I ever had a document to refer to with a description of every file (and every record layout in that file) in the system I was supporting, was mine (I'll get into that history later). Since I was the chief cook and bottle washer, I was able to maintain near perfect descriptions of each record layout for each file in the system.

Without the luxury of nice documentation, any time I want to know what file a particular variable is stored in, one way is to change that field in your test case and check the time stamp on all of the files associated with the application you are testing. That will at least narrow it down (hopefully) to a handful of possibilities. Identifying specific files can be valuable in the event you need to check for current version, for example, files that are part of a relational database.

Binary Hack

I like to save old compiled versions of the apps that I support. I'll save some as much as five years old, even from prior versions. This enables you to test old versions to see if the reported problem is a new problem, or if something broke somewhere along the line. If it's the latter, then establishing a timeline might help the programming staff find and fix the problem that much quicker. They may be able to correlate against any comments in the code, and maybe, you'll actually determine what happened instead of just throwing the thing into the mystery pile. Saving old versions are also useful in the event a customer, or the big boss wants to know why a certain feature is no longer available. Go back as far as you can and determine if that feature ever existed. CYB!

Okay, so what's a binary hack? If there are thirty old versions that somewhere a particular problem started occurring and you want to know which one, testing all thirty can be time consuming. Let's say the compile dates of these thirty range from January 2005 to December 2010. Begin testing with the one exactly in the middle, about December 2007. If what you are looking for fails, try an earlier version, but try the one exactly between January 2005 and December 2007 (about June 2006). Instead of testing each of the thirty archived versions, you're taking a shortcut and testing a fraction of them to arrive at exactly which one was the last not to fail. Of course, this is just one manual example, but this method is used for searching data by programs in much the same manner.

OMG, no Internet!

Upon losing your Internet connection, I recommend the following procedure:

Is it just one workstation, all workstations, and the server? If you don't know which wire or cable delivers your Internet service, then check all phone lines, cables, and power cords to make sure the cleaning folks didn't run over them with the vacuum cleaner. Cycle the power on firewalls, routers, and modems. (BTW, cycling the power on a hardware firewall doesn't guarantee its' been rebooted. You may have to reboot the firewall manually). If you still don't have service (check the server), restart the server. If you have access to the phone room, check the punch-down blocks for loose twisted pair. If you have T1 or better, run diagnostics on the NCIC. I try to have as much information as possible available before I call the Telco. This increases the chance that they can fix the problem from their office instead of sending a tech, which takes more time.

Over Heating

Overheated hard drives, mother boards, or video cards don't happen very often and are often overlooked as a potential cause of problems. The clue is usually when things don't make sense, for example, some applications run fine, others don't, and there is no discernable reason as to why. I had a situation where all of the customer's accounting applications were running fine. The application I supported at the time had intermittent problems, and coincidentally ran on top of a relational database engine. In this case, a side vent had become completely clogged which overheated the hard drive. Turns out it was just enough to knock out part the server installation of the engine. Everything was fine after I reinstalled it.

Many years ago, back in the days of CPM, I had to make a personal appearance at a customer site due to various problems with their computer.

Now, we need to put this into perspective: back in those days, a machine running CPM with 64kb of memory and a 2 mg hard drive cost about $30,000.00 – in 1980 dollars. For that kind of dough, I did house calls just to plug the thing back into the wall for the client. Anyway, this one took all of about a minute to figure out the problem. They had the CPU sitting on a north facing window sill, in direct sunlight. Ever read the specs on your hardware? Like operating temperatures for CRT monitors? Well, I also confirmed they start "popping" at about 95 degrees.

Restarts

Restarting Windows-based servers and workstations at least once a month, whether it appears necessary or not, is widely accepted throughout the industry. The Windows operating system is not known for its exemplary housekeeping abilities (allowing buildup of residual processes, maintaining locked records and files, and other anomalies which can all contribute to performance issues and other problems). I restart my machines regularly, not necessarily exactly once a month. You can usually tell when a specific machine needs restarting when network latency increases, or the machine begins to hang.

Running Client Applications on a Server

Unless the application is specific to managing the server or network, I never recommend installing any application which is otherwise intended for use by customer service or data entry personnel. Many commercial business software applications are referred to as "client-server" applications, where the client is synonymous with workstation. These applications, or programs, are installed and reside on each client, while the server "hosts" the data.

Thus, the server serves – its primary function is to remain "stand alone" for the purpose of achieving optimal network performance. And, from a security standpoint, it is never recommended that any user other than a network administrator be given access to a server.

Semantics and Terminology

Although I don't have control over message content generated by an operating system or third party application, I do suggest at every opportunity to the programming department, which I do have some control over, to scale down messages as a result of a given event. I see no reason to launch a screen sized window with a giant circled red "X" and a message exclaiming something like "Error – User Access Denied", when all that happens is more than one user is accessing the same record concurrently. You can bet every time this happens, you're going to get a call from a panicked user. There is a definite difference between a hard error message and an informative message. Both should be descriptive, but they shouldn't scare the bejegars out of the user.

Certain usage of terminology helps me mitigate inquires perceived to be a crisis by the user. Rather than using "bug" to refer to a problem, I use "issue". Instead of "fixing" the issue, I restate by saying the issue will be "corrected" or "repaired". When a user complains about an operational issue, which you know is by design, I suggest saying "I will submit your inquiry for further review".

Shortcut Icons

Twice in over fifteen years have I actually seen a corrupted short cut icon.

By that I mean launching an application via a short cut icon which produced different results than launching the same application the shortcut was pointing to by double clicking the ".exe". I have no clue to this day as to cause, but recreating the icon resolved the issue at the time. I suppose one of the advanced items in the properties (like running in separate memory) could have had something to do with it. One simple rule when troubleshooting is not to run the application via the shortcut unless you think there is a problem with it.

Software Firewalls

Especially when attempting to run legacy applications, software firewalls often contribute to a host or problems. Good old "GPF's" (General Protection Faults, and for you who remember, aka "Blue Screen of Death" back in the DOS days), are typical with this mix. One of first places I go when troubleshooting GPF's and other hard errors which refer to dll's and the registry, is to disable any software firewall long enough to determine if it's the source of the problem. By the way, as I have mentioned in my section about antivirus apps, the same kind of error scenario applies.

System Performance Issues

Is the loss of performance just with a particular application, or are other applications such as email, spreadsheet, or your general ledger accounting system also experiencing slower responses? Are all workstations affected, or just one particular workstation? This is typically a performance issue that should be brought to the attention of the IT department. Here are some suggestions as to what to look for:

Check hard drive space on all workstations and servers (see "What, Hard Drives Run Out of Space?).

Defragment all hard drives.

Run virus scans.

Run spyware scans.

Check Event Viewers and any/all other network logs on workstations and servers for any potential hardware and software problems.

Delete Temporary Internet files on all workstations (and servers).

Confirm that Internet radios or streaming videos are kept to a minimum.

Confirm that all wireless hardware is working properly. Restart all servers and workstations.

Configure antivirus apps to limit real time scanning.

Consider load balancing. Have they loaded every conceivable app on one server instead of dedicating apps equally across multiple servers?

Good luck with peer-to-peer networks. Get them to invest in a dedicated server.

I have found the time it takes to delete Temporary Internet files is directly proportional to the degradation of performance of a given machine. I have seen this process take as long as thirty minutes. Deleting Temporary Internet files is one of the first places I go when I get a squawk about slow machines.

Event Viewers and other network related log files on servers and workstations should be reviewed periodically for potential problems with the network. Network packet collisions, broadcast storms, even multiple users downloading Windows Updates at the same time can cause performance problems on a network. IT personnel should monitor these issues as a matter of procedure and preventative maintenance.

Thrashing is a relatively older term referring to when the resources creating and managing a time slice ended up taking more time than the time slice itself, resulting in nothing actually executing. Thrashing was typically managed by the system administrator on mid-sized mainframes of the 1970's. Time slices were based on a user's priority. Programmers supporting senior engineers and scientists would tend to be granted a larger time slice (more of the mainframe's CPU time) than a student. I use the definition of thrashing to describe network latency where load balancing has obviously been overlooked.

What Has No Teeth and Eats Floppies?

A few brief stories on the lighter side:

This one goes back a ways, remember how PC's had dual 5 ¼ inch floppy drives stacked one on top of the other? I had one guy (actually a VP who headed up the entire product development department) insert a 5 ¼ inch floppy, not in the drive, but in the space in between the floppy drives! Guess who had to crack the case and fetch the disk out?

One time, a guy left the 5 ¼ inch non-bootable floppy in the A: drive overnight. The power had failed causing that PC to attempt to reboot. The PC was unable to successfully reboot, so it cycled throughout the night.

Next morning, the floppy had turned into road kill, the otherwise oxidized surface of the boot track was gone.

I was verbally walking a user through an install using 5 ¼ inch floppies. I told the user to insert the first of the series of floppies into the floppy drive and close the door (remember the little lever, or "door" that you had to close to secure the floppy disk in the drive?). He got up and closed his office door. And then asked me why I told him to do so.

What, Hard Drives Run Out of Space?

Yes. Even though 100gb+ hard drives are the norm today, it doesn't take very many videos, pictures, presentations, and archived databases to fill a 100gb hard drive. Although the problem of running out of disk space is not as prevalent as in the past, it still happens and it can still be very destructive. I have seen many commercial applications that do not check for available disk space. Makes me think again about how some people are able to survive.

Based on my experience, 30% or less available disk space is the threshold where you should start getting concerned about performance degradation. Good file management practices will help make it easier to administrate and organize your files and folders that reside on your hard drive. For example, never save exported data files, spreadsheets, or word processing documents into an applications' installation or data folder. Most applications maintain themselves. You should direct your users never delete or rename any file in an application's installation or data folder. The reason I bring it up is because I have seen it done.

Chapter 10 Periodic Maintenance

Periodic Maintenance (PM, aka Preventative Maintenance) is a term that implies maintaining equipment at reasonable intervals as a preventative measure against equipment failure. My goal has been to achieve better than 98% network uptime, not counting planned downtime, for all network components.

Cheap versus Frugal

I plead guilty to buying generic brands of some products. It just depends on what type of product you are buying. For example, generic brand batteries (for use on anything) have to be way up on my "NO" list. The old adage "you get what you pay for" is something I believe in. Generic light bulbs, packing tape, and glue are a few examples of items I would stay away from. However, consumables such as paper towels, paper plates, plastic cups and tableware, who cares? You're going to use them once and throw it all away. The same concept applies to office supplies, replacement cartridges, and storage media.

I'm using batteries as an example because I've probably seen more grief on this topic alone. Although some may argue while generic batteries are more cost effective than brand names, and by some accounts last only about 70%, yet cost less than half of a brand name, they forget to factor in the time and hassle of ordering and replacing batteries. And, the margin for error resulting in breakage increases every time you have to change out even something as trivial as a battery. I believe it is essential that quality is considered as the highest priority for items such as backup media, packaging for shipment of media, toner cartridges, and printer paper.

Another example of an attempt to save on cost is buying separate components and building your computer from scratch. While building your own is a wonderful hobby, ordering a brand name to your exact specifications is always the better option cost-wise. And your do-it-yourself project isn't going to include much, if any, of a warranty.

There are exceptions. Common sense is going to (hopefully) dictate whether you spend $15.00 generic or $150.00 brand name for the same set of cables for your new $800.00 flat screen (I'd go with the $15.00 set). Or, if you're trying to nurse some old equipment until your next budget is approved, you may not have a choice but to buy a non-OEM power supply or tape transport.

I recall an experience regarding a relatively expensive copy machine which the management wanted to keep. The machine was a well known brand name, had been reasonable maintained, about half way through it's' life cycle, and was still very much cost effective. Then came the recession of late 2000's. They ordered a generic replacement for the toner cartridge saving about $30.00 or so. The generic cartridge didn't fit exactly as the OEM cartridge. Someone took a sharp object and attempted to make it fit. Then the whole thing was dumped on me to resolve. Well, by that time the entire internal mechanisms of the machine had been saturated with toner. The area where the toner cartridge attached had been severely damaged. A total loss is usually defined as when an item costs less to replace than to repair.

One of the dumbest projects I have ever been assigned involved building our own battery packs that powered the door locks in the building. This type of door lock are known as Proximity Locks, and can be programmed to limit access throughout a building.

The Management at the time decided to install the less expensive individual lock instead of running power and data to each door. The latter would have meant having a clean interface via a Management Console to control each point of entry around the clock. The former meant I had to reprogram each lock every time a battery pack failed. Which meant I had to dedicate a laptop with the pre-programmed employee and guest data and make sure I maintained a backup copy on the LAN. The battery packs were simply four "AA's" wired in series, and one pack lasted about a month. And the batteries weren't the only component to fail. The cost in overhead maintaining the less expensive version of this rubber band and paper clip system would have paid for the premium system in just a few years. Oh, I almost forgot; the idea of building our own battery packs was scrubbed when they figured out it cost less to buy the OEM replacements.

This is the dumbest attempt at trying to save money by recouping losses for damaged equipment due to alleged negligence by the carrier. One of my side duties at a small distribution firm was to maintain the RMA (Return Materials Authorization) database and to make sure customers and our regional sales representatives were getting quality repairs to their equipment in a reasonable amount of time. While damage to equipment during shipment was the responsibility of the customer, damaged equipment belonging to the company was another story. Management insisted I recover monies for all damaged product from the carrier no matter what it cost in terms of my time. It took as much as eight hours of my time to get credited $30.00 (our retail price) for a part which cost us perhaps $5.00. And there was no guarantee the carrier would pay. Just didn't make sense to me since my salary was a good bit more than $4.75 an hour.

ESD Safe

ESD stands for electrostatic discharge". ESD safe equipment, such as solder equipment and even portable vacuums are designed to reduce electrostatic discharge, thereby reducing potential damage to the electronics. If you support in-house hardware, investing in an ESD safe portable vacuum will be one of the best decisions you'll ever make. Then use it. Keeping printers and other hardware clean will increase operational life, save on repair costs, and save you headaches.

Note: I like to keep my own personal set of screw drivers, nut drivers, a few wrenches, a couple of sets of pliers, and a measuring tape handy just in case. Even better, a multi-tool is the best hand tool purchase I've made in twenty years. Oh, don't forget to include a small flashlight in your tool kit. And, save those straws from disposed cans of spray lubricant and compressed air. Once in a while they tend to get separated and lost from the new cans.

Printer Maintenance

Granted, this one might seem bit excessive-compulsive, but I go so far as to keep paper trays full. I carefully fan the paper, reset the paper guides, and gently but firmly place the paper in the tray taking care to align properly. You wouldn't believe how many times some wing nut tries to cram a whole ream of paper into a tray designed to hold less than a ream, only to have it jam. And, who gets the call to fix it? That would be you.

By the way, one really obscure problem that might come up and is sometimes referred to as "contrast reversal". I had a user who received PDF's from Japan that would more often than not print black background and white foreground.

Somehow, printing the document would change the printer settings, which I would have to reset manually via the printer console. Thought I'd share this one with you, just in case.

Maintenance Logs

I prefer maintaining logs for each piece of equipment for purposes of recording maintenance performed, errors, repairs, and tracking consumption of consumables such as toner cartridges. Maintenance logs are a CYB thing. You may have to prove to the boss you have changed the toner cartridge regularly and before the cartridge went completely dry. Letting toner cartridges go dry can cause damage to the drum, a dollar amount closer to the cost of a new printer rather than the fractional amount of the cost for cartridge. Maintenance logs can help with maintaining inventory on consumables as well. Tracking how often a particular color printer needs a black and white versus a color cartridge gives you some idea how many cartridges to have on hand. You don't want the marketing department's favorite color printer to run out of ink half way through a print run, only to find out you don't have a replacement.

If your company leases equipment, logs come in handy to determine the overall cost of consumables. When the lease is up, you may consider replacement with more efficient equipment with the goal of cutting the cost of consumables. By logging dates and times, you may be able to determine a pattern nailing down the cause. For example, you may find issues with your UPS may coincide with failure of switches, routers, or NICs. Or, phone systems that fail every time there is a heavy period of rain. I've experienced the latter, I finally was able to convince the Telco that a B-Box adjacent to the building was flooding, causing catastrophic failure of the phone system.

Plan to crack the cases of all workstations and servers once a year to thoroughly clean and vacuum, and pay particularly close attention to cooling fans and vents. Keeping cables routed away from any vicinity where they can be disturbed by in-house personnel and cleaning crews will help reduce problems, not only with broken cabling, but connectors as well.

PM is not limited to exclusively hardware. Use of tools to regularly monitor the network can alert you to potential problems before network components go down. I would review event viewers and other management console apps at least once a week just to keep an eye on things. If the Server Administrator app tells you one of your redundant power supplies has failed, replace it as soon as possible. There is a reason for redundancy, figure both power supplies are the same age. If one goes, the other is sure to follow soon.

Software Updates

There are many cases for argument on when and how often to install updates for just about anything. Whether updating operating systems, mission critical applications, or just printer drivers, there is always a potential for disaster because the source, or provider, of the update messed up big time. I once lost our multi-media machine due to a "routine" operating system update containing changes to a foreign language translator. Cost me an entire weekend rebuilding that machine. On another occasion, uninstalling a bad update from a major supplier of UPS's repaired an entire LAN. And there's the time a major supplier of antivirus software released an update that sent tens of thousands of workstations into "endless-loop" restarts. The bottom line is, depending on the specific update, I favor a "cooling off" period. Let someone else who didn't buy my guide and read it to learn the hard way.

And then there is the matter of how to deploy all of these updates. I never allow a server operating system to automatically update. First, it breaks my rule about the cooling off period, and second, I can't trust that the server won't just restart, or worse, shutdown, on its' own during peak business hours. Workstations aren't as critical, I allow updates to download automatically, but I do not allow them to install automatically. I never push updates over the network. Too many times an update fails to install, and fails to notify me of the fact that it didn't install. I take the extra time to install each application on each workstation ensuring a successful installation. This may not work as standard procedure in all shops, however, I recommend this approach if you are managing a relatively small LAN. Obviously, it's just not practical to manually install everything on larger LAN's.

Trouble with Printers

Infamous "Missing Printers" Call

Another day, another panic call. Our multi-media guy "lost" all of his printers. He was in one his web applications attempting to print a document but couldn't find any of his printers. He called and ordered me to his office immediately. Well, this one took me a little longer, about five seconds, to realize that all he had to do was scroll to the left in the window containing the list of printers.

And while most printer problems aren't going to be as easy to remedy as the one I just described, the following is a list of "to-do" items in the event you are unable to print reports or a screen shot from a workstation:

1. Printing issues typically occur when a new workstation or new printer is deployed. If your applications have separate printer configuration settings, then check each workstation to confirm the default printer is set to the same default printer for that workstation as in Start, Settings, Printers and Faxes. Make sure you can print a test page from the printer's properties tab, and confirm that printing from another application (e.g. a text file) is successful.

2. If you are still unable to print, delete the default printer and re-define the default printer for the workstation. Then re-define the default printer in your application. Try reinstalling the printer driver, and use a generic one or an older version driver for that particular make and model. Try resetting the default printer to another printer, then back again. Try shutting down all printers, workstations, and servers. Turn on in this order: printers, servers, and workstations. Printers (like servers) should not be turned off for any reason other than repair, maintenance, or physically moving the printer.

3. One clue with this type of problems is: "it was working great yesterday, it's not working today". So what has changed in the past twenty four hours with the printers, printer drivers, or the print server on the network that could be causing problems? Is this a problem which occurs with only one workstation, or does it happen with all workstations? If the problem is with just one workstation then what's different about this workstation's printer configuration versus the other workstations?

My experience, particularly with legacy applications, the application communicates with printers through a standard interface to the operating system. Printers assigned to user defined ports that don't exist in an attempt to work around printer issues with other applications can also cause printing problems.

Problems may also occur with locally shared printers not having appropriate access rights. Legacy applications tend to not support Print from Print Preview, or duplex printing. Although rare, I've actually seen applications fail if no printers are installed. Before printing labels, print a test page using a doc labeled "test" on top, with an arrow indicating direction of the feed. Stick one for each printer in a binder for future reference.

I once experienced an interesting problem with a user getting General Protection Faults when running some of the applications I supported at the time. The GPF error mentioned a specific DLL, a rarity in itself. The applications that were failing all had to do with reports and only occurred on one out of a dozen or so workstations. I did an Internet search on the DLL and found it was 64 bit specific. The user's LAN was 32 bit native. I set the default printer for that workstation to another printer and everything worked fine. I advised the user to inform her IT department of the issue. Stuff like this never ceases to amaze me.

Tip: Although not a common occurrence, legacy applications will fail if there are no printers installed, or if there isn't one defined as the default printer. You may also experience viewable reports failing as well since some legacy applications use print controllers that also drive the graphics for viewable reports. I have also seen legacy applications fail due to printer names that are too long.

Label Challenged

Based on my own experience, most users don't know that most common printers technically do not support printing labels. This is especially true for the laser jets.

If a label should become stuck to the drum, you're out the cost of a new drum, likely as much as a new printer by the time you pay someone to install it. RTFM, and make sure the printer you want to use is rated for labels.

My little trick for remembering which way to insert labels into the paper tray, is to draw an arrow in the direction the paper is fed from the paper tray. Then print a test page, with the words literally "Test Page". I refer to the test page for a given printer if I can't remember which way the labels go.

This label challenged user called with this question: "My labels are supposed to print 3 across and ten down, why are they only printing 3 across and 8 down with a bunch of space at the bottom?". I instructed her to check the printer configuration. Turns out the printer had been reconfigured to print on special size paper, probably for brochures. She changed the printer configuration to print on standard sized paper.

Chapter 11 Ensuring Data Integrity

This is a common question I get from customers, although they use different terminology, and the responses in this chapter apply not only to the applications you support for your customers, but to all of your corporate data including word processing documents, spreadsheets, and data from general ledger accounting systems.

Many software applications maintain databases with hundreds, even thousands of specific data fields inside hundreds or thousands of. Most applications employ "data validation" as an integral part of basic design. For example, a user cannot enter a city or a state in a field that expects a numeric value. Zip codes are verified against a zip code database upon entry to ensure the zip code is valid. Pre-defined tables such as those for state abbreviations insure these field values are entered correctly and consistently each and every time. Data validation and pre-defined tables are just a couple of features that increase and maintain the integrity of data. There are many possible events which may occur that can cause damage to files or databases:

1) Deletion or renaming of database files

Most applications are self maintained within their own folders. Basic file maintenance procedures should include the creation of separate folders for storing exported data, word processing documents, and spreadsheets. This minimizes the possibility of tampering with an application's critical files.

2) Restoration of archived backups over current production files and databases

Occasionally, an archived backup may need to be restored for auditing purposes or to simply retrieve a selected file. Care must be taken not to restore historical data over current production data (that may not be currently backed up) resulting in loss of data.

3) Viruses

Fortunately, viruses have played a less significant role with respect to loss or corruption of data in recent years. This can be attributed to better informed users and IT departments, and better virus protection hardware and software. However, complacency can throw this right out the door. Check periodically to make sure anti-virus software and virus definitions are always up to date.

4) Network failure due to hardware or software application issues

Network reliability has increased dramatically within the past several years. Data loss or corruption due to network failure is relatively rare. But, there are events that arise where Event Viewers and other network maintenance logs and tools may need to be referenced to locate the source of the problem. Broadcast storms, packet losses, and even the failure of an analog switch (I've seen this one a couple times) are potential causes of data loss and data corruption.

5) Server or Workstation failure due to hardware or software application issues

Hardware reliability has also increased over the past several years and data loss due to faulty hardware is not as common.

However, as with any machine containing moving parts, maintenance plays an important role. Periodic cleaning of workstations and servers can prevent air ducts from clogging which can cause over-heating and failure of hardware components.

Generally, you can't anticipate occurrences of specific problems which may cause damage to your data. I did once successfully predict a hard drive crash on a user's workstation. I was checking the Event Viewer and recognized a series of severe errors. I don't recall the error description, but I did inform the user of the impending disaster. Of course nothing about it, and the drive crashed two weeks later. The best possible solution to maintaining data integrity is a regularly scheduled and enforced procedure for full backups of all data. In short, backing up is the best insurance against data loss.

Time for a break, this story goes back a ways, but it's still entertaining and is a great example of common sense, or lack thereof. This event takes place back in the days when hard drives were the size of washing machines. The "disk packs" as they were known, were about the size of a compact spare tire, loaded from the top of the drive, seated, and bolted. By the way, each pack had about 200mb capacity, and each drive cost around $80,000, not too shabby for 1979. Anyway, a fellow named Jim was an NC programmer and worked the second shift. He came to work one evening, took his pack from the storage rack and proceeded to load into one of the drives. Hmmm, it didn't boot, so Jim tried reseating the pack. Still didn't boot. Jim installed it onto another drive. Still didn't boot.

Five drives later someone realized Jim had migrated in succession a bad pack causing each drives' heads to crash. I recall the price tag was around five grand apiece to repair the drives. I would've given Jim a break if he would have realized what was going on after the second drive failed. Maybe even the third one. But five?

Chapter 12 File Importing

Do you support applications that require importing of data? If so, then you know what a pain it can be to get the user to understand basic concepts on file formats. Let me fill you in on another shocker: professional data vendors – guys who scrub data for a living – often don't get it right either, especially if you support legacy applications. Don't be surprised if they don't know what fixed length fields are!

True story: I had a very upset client call to report that 80,000 blank records had been created in the accounting application as a result of importing a file he'd received from a telemarketer he hired. As you know, since 99.99% of all problems related to importing data are caused by the data itself, I asked him to send me the file he imported. You got it – every one of the 80,000 records contained 100 commas, nothing else, just commas! This user didn't even bother to look at the file before importing. And, I wish I had a buck for each time data didn't get backed up BEFORE importing. Anyway, importing records is a great time-saver and a vital component to many database applications. Here I discuss a few tips for improving your users' file import success.

Delimiters

There is only one comment I can make regarding delimiters. And that is to watch out for characters embedded inside delimited fields where the character is the same as the delimiter. I've seen many a legacy app allow this to happen. Look for this when reviewing any file for import.

Review the File

Most unsuccessful imports can be traced to a problem with the contents of the import file such as corrupted or invalid records and characters, missing data, or improperly formatted data. It is for these reasons that it is important to always open and review the records before attempting to import the file.

How do you determine if the file's content has a problem? You might be inclined to simply open it in Excel. Hold on! While Excel is an excellent tool, it formats each cell based on content and can potentially mask any otherwise visible problems with data in the file. An excellent example is zip codes for eastern seaboard states that have leading zeros. Unlike Excel, Notepad will display the file's "raw" contents without any formatting.

A classic example of a major error as a result of not reviewing a spreadsheet prior to import is when the spreadsheet contains an empty column. The unsuspecting user assumes the entire sheet is sorted, for example, by zip code. However, the empty column following the zip code field causes the remaining columns not to be included in the sort. So, the phone numbers, email addresses, and other data beyond the empty column are now out of sync with the rest of the data. You might be surprised how often this happens.

Use Notepad or WordPad to open text files. If it's a ".csv", change the extension to ".txt" (if it's an Excel file, save to a ".csv "). Look for unintelligible words or garbage characters. Look for empty records (e.g. blank spots between other records) or empty fields, such as a missing Last Name field. If you see any problems, you can attempt to correct them yourself but this may lead to other problems if you are not very careful.

If the list was rented or purchased, have your user contact the vendor and explain what you see. If it is an internal list and your user is not comfortable with database manipulation, suggest they work closely with an IT professional who can assist them in cleaning things up.

Summary

If you receive a ".csv" file, I recommend viewing it using Notepad by changing the extension to ".txt". Any major anomalies should be readily visible as you scroll down the file. Remember Excel has the potential to format cells which may mask any potential problems which is why I never recommend importing Excel files as standard procedure. I like Access, it's a decent tool, and it doesn't have a lot of the limitations that Excel has. But remember when you make a change in Access, it saves it real time.

Always Back Up – Save your users potentially hours of grief and frustration by reminding them at every opportunity to always back up their data before importing any records. I recommend every correspondence with a user regarding import data include a reminder to back up their data. Because when they don't, and something goes south, you have CYB'd yourself!

Careful mapping fields; emphasize the importance to your user of paying attention to field mappings. I had one instance where the user mapped the last name to the First Name field and the first name to the Last Name field. Guess what call came into my office? Uh huh, they couldn't find anyone they'd imported by their last name. OMG, they're all gone, where'd they go?

At some point you might get directly involved with designing the import file itself. An example would be a file from a website containing names, addresses, and demographics. I have found the best way to communicate to the user as to what fields will be necessary for importing into the app that you support, is to have them look at the data fields they use for manual entry. What could be simpler than to hand the web developer a screen shot of the data entry screen and tell him these are the fields I need to import. If you're a web developer by trade, I apologize, but while most web developers perform a great job bringing up all that eye candy for the world to see, they don't know squat about what is necessary for the rest of the operation.

Tip: Legacy applications may have problems either reading, writing, importing, or exporting using long filenames. If you suspect a problem using a long filename, rename the file in question to an 8.3 format

Chapter 13 Data Conversions

If you are supporting a commercially available application, you no doubt have competitors, and odds are you already know all about how much "fun" data conversions are. Especially data from legacy applications that have little or no data validation. If you can read the data, that's a good start. Now all you need to do is figure out file structures, record formats and, you probably need to know what the data is. As in "What is this date for?", "is this a bill-to or ship-to address?". Among the most prevalent problems with non-validated data are alpha characters residing in numeric fields, resolving dates, the letter "O" versus zero, and my personal favorite: "Where are the leading zeros on those zip codes for eastern seaboard states?".

Most of the commercially available applications that I have supported require a data conversion from a customer's existing application. This is the most critical part of the post-sales process for a new client. I recommend spending an appropriate amount of quality time to educate the new client with the details of what a data conversion entails. One important tool I recommend is a data conversion questionnaire with generalized questions regarding the database to be converted. Some of the questions included could be:

1) Is the data to be converted from a commercially available application (competitor), administrated by a service bureau, or developed by an in-house IT department?
2) What format will the data files to be converted be in (.csv, .txt., .mdb)?
3) Will the data to be converted be accompanied by documentation describing the file and record structures?

4) How many customer name and address records are currently in your application's database?

5) Will there be a report set available for each iteration of conversion passes for purposes of reconciliation?

The first question should tip you off immediately as to what kind of nightmare you'll be facing. I'm not sure which is worse, legacy or in-house systems. If it's a competitor, the data is probably going to be in good shape but proprietary documentation might be difficult to obtain. Hopefully, questions 2 and 3 will take some of the edge off that nightmare. 4 and 5 will allow you to compare results from the conversion to your application against what appears in the customer's old system. Reconciling record counts and any accounting between the two systems will give you an idea about the accuracy of the converted results.

Conversion Guidelines

As part of the user's education, I recommend including documentation describing file formats and record structures. The following is a good example:

"A record layout describes each field and its position within a file. Some fields will be obvious, such as name and address information, but many will not. If any fields contain special codes, describe each code and its meaning. The preferred method is to document and provide data for only those fields that are currently being used, saving considerable time during the conversion process. The following describes popular file formats in order of preference:

1. Access (".mdb"); Microsoft Access file.

2. ASCII, comma-delimited, quote-comma delimited, tab delimited (".txt", ".csv"); Other special characters may be used as delimiters if necessary. However, the delimiter character must not appear in the data. Tabs are the preferred delimiter.

3. dbase IV (*.dbf); Export as ASCII, if possible. If not, do not modify any field or record attributes.

4. ASCII, fixed length: Also referred to as fixed field or table. All records in the file are equal in length, all fields within each record are fixed length.

5. Excel (*.xls); Microsoft Excel file.

6. Other; .Notify our Technical Support Department for details".

Conversion Process

Explain to the customer that interim passes of data conversion may contain inaccuracies, and will therefore be necessary to reconvert resulting in the delivery of another pass of converted data. During this time, the new users should take advantage of familiarizing themselves with the new application by entering fictitious (or real) data and generating reports. Make sure the user knows that any test data entered into preliminary, or draft, versions may be overwritten by an updated pass of converted data. Despite efforts to achieve the greatest possible accuracy, there may be unforeseen issues that will arise which need special attention. These types of issues are common in systems that have limited or no data validation. The following is a list of examples of such issues:

1. "O"s (letter O) and "0"s (number zero) embedded mixed in the same field.

2. "l"s (letter l) and "1"s (number one) embedded mixed in the same field.

3. "z"s (letter z) and "2"s (number two) embedded mixed in the same field.

4. Data in free formatted systems may not distinguish between Blank (ASCII 32) and null (ASCII 0) characters.

5. Leading zeros can be dropped on east coast zip codes (Excel files containing east cost zip codes can drop the leading zeros if not formatted properly). I've seen the letter "O" substituted for the leading zero presumably because the legacy application was unable to handle leading zeros.

6. Fields containing full names should be broken down into individual components. The following examples may not convert to a legible single first name and last name:

    a. "The families of Mr. and Mrs. Michael James Johnson and Mr. and Mrs. Robert Douglas Smith"
    b. "Julie Hall / John Hunter"
    c. "Mr. & Mrs. William Olsen & Family"
    d. "Whispering Pines Bed and Breakfast"

Confirm all information provided in the data conversion questionnaire matches what is defined in the customers' present system. The customers' data will be converted based on the information provided. If the information provided is different than what is actually defined in your present system, the resulting conversion may not match.

Testing the Conversion

Running parallel systems for a month or two is usually preferred by the new customer.

My preference is to "drop the curtain" and go live with your application as soon as possible, even if it means not running parallel. Of course I have always had the luxury of letting the customer know that if something is missed down the road, my programming department can always write a utility to fix incorrectly converted data, or add any data that was missed as a result of the conversion process.

Testing every record in every file is obviously not feasible. I recommend checking several dozen or so at the beginning (e.g. lowest record numbers), a few dozen or so in the middle, and a dozen at the end. Consider the following areas when checking for discrepancies:

1. Is the customer's full name separated into the honorific, first and last name fields?

2. For U.S. customers, are the state, zip code, and phone information converted correctly?

3. For Canadian customers, are the province and postal codes converted correctly?

4. Verify monies due and all historical payment data.

5. Are bill-to and ship-to addresses, if applicable, being converted?

6. Are multiple orders linked to the correct customer record?

7. Are the accounts receivable and accounts payable accurate? I recommend running all appropriate reports on both the old system and the new application for purposes of comparing these numbers for accuracy.

Final Delivery

The most difficult part of the conversion from aside from all of the issues already described is "dropping the curtain", or delivering the final product. Users are always hesitant to make the big switch, letting go of that 15 year old DOS application for the shiny new 21st century system. Concern about the accuracy of the data and potential problems down the road often cause users to procrastinate. Your boss wants to pull the switch as soon as possible, assuming the conversion is reasonably accurate, perhaps within plus or minus a half a percent. You and I are, as usual, are in the middle of no-man's land. We must deliver a quality product to the customer, and deliver it in a timely basis to keep the boss happy. By the way, one reason the boss likes to get customers on board asap is to insure all of the contractual obligations are met. "Refund" is not in the boss' vocabulary. The other reason is the sooner a new client gets aboard, the sooner the invoice of next years' subscription support can be sent.

I use a technique, referred to earlier in this guide, as providing a "warm fuzzy" feeling to the customer. It's an attempt at gaining the customer's confidence in the final product. My pitch to the customer is if, for any reason we find that data was missed in the conversion process, we can always write a utility to import that missing data based on the data provided for the original conversion. And, I make this offer whether we find a problem weeks, months, even a year after delivery. In most cases this extended offer takes the edge off the customer's hesitance to move forward. Of course, I have had the luxury of some authority over the programming department allowing me to extend an offer like this.

Your policies may differ, but I highly recommend this technique as the potential is there to improve cash flow, certainly a selling point when approaching your boss.

Chapter 14 Recommending System Requirements

The first requirement is to ensure that your new hardware will arrive intact. Read on:

The Bigger the Fragile Sticker, the Harder the Fall

This one's funny now, but it certainly wasn't back then: I was on my way back from lunch one day and pulling into the garage at the office when I noticed about four or five guys trying to unload a refrigerator-freezer sized crate from the back of a bobtail truck. I noticed the crate had the logo of a well known manufacturer of mini-mainframes of the time. I suddenly realized it was for delivery to my employer. Now, I have no idea why the truck wasn't equipped with a lift since the crate weighed four to five hundred pounds, but before I could intervene (I was a manager at this company and had the authority), the knuckleheads managed to drop the brand new Sun about four feet to the concrete to the tune of about $350,000.00 (1987 dollars). The machine was a total loss for someone, not us though.

The following is a basic boilerplate guide that I often use when making recommendations on system requirements. Obviously, different applications will have different requirements. I like to simplify because it lessens the intimidation factor for prospective clients:

Absolutely never recommend Joe's Computer Store around the corner, or custom built hardware from any vendor other than a name brand.

129

Custom built machines are often more expensive, and you don't know how long Joe will be around the corner to support your hardware investment. Name brand vendors offer long term warranties against defect, and relatively inexpensive extended warranty plans (which I highly recommend).

Servers and Workstations should arrive bundled with the latest OS and service packs, and the entire physical hard drive should be partitioned as the local drive. This is an argument that you must not lose. Partitioning a hard drives for the OS and apps on the local drive with the intention of partitioning the remaining space on a different logical drive for data is a an old school preferred configuration. I'd like a buck for every time a local drive has run out of space after a year because of lack of forward planning. I find it easier to create and share folders on a large partition for different applications for purposes of controlling access and performing backups rather than maintain multiple partitions. And, as I mentioned in the section of hot-swappable hard drives, never configure a partition across multiple physical drives.

1. Server(s) should also arrive with the latest OS and service packs. Horsepower is the name of the game here, so maximize ram and hard drive size. Dual NICs, dual power supplies, and mirrored array for redundancy is highly recommended.

2. Uninterrupted power supplies (UPS's) are recommended (but should be required)for all workstations and servers.

3. A backup system. Tape or other suitable method. I detail back up methods and procedures elsewhere in this guide. And, it should be standard operating procedure.

4. Hardware firewall. Not software firewalls.

5. Name brand Anti-virus and Anti-Spyware, never use shareware or free applications.

6. At least one workstation equipped with a DVD burner.

Chapter 15 Professional Courtesies

Professional courtesies not only reinforce confidence and trust between the customer and vendor, but they can also serve as a value added service. Yet another reason for the customer to continue their subscription to support contracts, purchase training, and purchase products.

Depending on the circumstances (in other words, how cheap is the customer, and do they pay on time?), offer tutorials within your means and relevance to the products you support for third party apps such as spreadsheets and word processors. Perhaps a review on how to prepare files for importing as covered in this guide, or provide some house cleaning services (straighten out the files within the scope of the apps you support). Remember to Make Yourself Valuable. As far as I'm concerned, the management at your organization considers you a necessary evil, a cost of doing business. Walking into the boss' office with a credit card number for the purchase of that new ecommerce module by an existing customer will help change that persona. I am not saying you have to be a salesman on top of all the rest of the stuff you deal with, I am suggesting taking advantage of a sales situation should it occur.

When connecting online to a customer, stay out of the domain (literally and figuratively) of another administrator's network. Always obtain permission (preferably an email so you effectively have it in writing) before making any changes involving issues outside of the scope of your responsibilities. Put yourself in that administrator's shoes, you don't want someone you don't know touching your stuff.

Upon completing a session after the user you are supporting has already left for the day, shut down or lock their workstation, and delete the remote entry connection. This is not only just a courtesy, this is for security purposes and CYB. After all, who's going to get the call in the event of something malicious happens after you are the last one logged in?

In the event you still have an established connection with a user from a prior session, I recommend always getting permission from that user before re-connecting. Although it is tempting to get in and complete your task, you don't want to be put in a position where you connect in and have somebody's confidential information on the screen.

Always report problems at your customers' end. This includes disconnected phone or fax, bounced email, web site issues, and any changes in their physical address.

Make sure they are aware that their subscription to support is about to expire and let them know that without it, you are not able to provide any assistance. Propose to do some custom programming at no charge if the customer re-ups early on their subscription support. Suggest additional training in the event of personnel turnover. Evaluate their Standard Operating Procedures (SOP) to see if they might take advantage of utilization of existing products, or purchase of additional products and services that will increase their bottom line.

Never use the customers' 800 number when calling back for support if they are current on their subscription support contract.

House Cleaning

Always back everything up before doing any house cleaning. Depending on the quality of the customer, I offer to perform house cleaning within the folders for the applications that I support. This might include organizing all spreadsheets, word processing documents, and exported flat files into each of their own folders. My goal is generally to keep the application data and application installation folders clean. This is another method that discourages users from getting into dedicated data folders and inadvertently deleting required files. Yes, I have had this happen. A user decides to delete files critical to the application without any knowledge of what the files' function is, thus bringing the application to it's' knees.

One organization I worked for had two divisions, PC applications (me), and the mainframe applications division. The customer support staff in the mainframe division decided to perform some house cleaning. Not backing up before house cleaning cost them six months work. They obviously weren't doing complete backups of everything, Ironically, they wouldn't have found out had they not done the housecleaning in the first place.

Visitors

I have worked mostly in casual dress environments, so I advise any visiting clients that casual attire is appropriate. However, my attire becomes formal for visiting prospective clients. In addition to any lunch arrangements, I also have on hand hot coffee, sodas, juices, fruit, and maybe some granola bars. A small investment can yield a big return.

Chapter 16 Liaison with other Members of Technical Staff

A Couple of Programmer's Nightmares

I have run across even the most seasoned programmers that can't grasp the concept of the difference between running a compiled application versus running the application in a development studio. The nightmare situation is when a compiled app fails, yet it runs successfully inside the development studio. This precludes the programmer from one of his most powerful tools – the ability to step through code to locate the specific line on which the application fails. Unfortunately, the only recourse is to enter debug statements, recompile, and run until the specific line of code that is failing is found by process of elimination.

Nightmare on top of nightmare is when the problem goes away after a debug statement has been entered and the application recompiled. The added debug statement causes the stack to change, and will most likely cause the application to fail somewhere else. There is no elegant method of resolving this WCS (Worst Case Scenario). He's just going to have to earn his paycheck on this one.

Note: "Spaghetti" code is usually to blame for this type of catastrophic failure. As applications evolve, many programmers might add or change code using their own "technique" instead of adhering to design standards that were originally set forth. Defining variables that are meaningless as a descriptor of what the variable is, lack of comments in the code, not checking for overflow of array boundaries, and not checking for zero divisors before a divide operation are typical examples of sloppy coding.

Maintaining spaghetti code requires what I refer to as "Surgical Programming". I consider the programmers who inherit spaghetti code and are actually able to make successful and reliable repairs and updates to be among the finest in the business.

Internet Use at the Office

This topic is similar to the Air Conditioning Wars described earlier in this guide. It's part of company politics and a Catch 22 at the same time.

Company polices regarding "personal" Internet use during office hours differ widely. Most of my employers just left the whole issue alone, allowing the IT department to grant unlimited access, or in problem situations to use discretion when limiting access. I agree with this type of open policy. Policing in-house users becomes an administrative burden on the IT department. Besides, department managers should have a clue as to the productivity of the employees they manage. One example of a disadvantage to the open policy allows users to download apps that can contain potential threats to the network.

The other end of the spectrum is to lock down Internet use user by user based on their specific requirements. This is a policy that eats into the resources of the IT department. A small company with a couple hundred users might mean policy changes on a daily basis. What a waste of time. Management is supposed hire quality employees which should prevent this type of abuse in the first place.

As an Assistant Manager of IT, I was asked for my opinion on how to reduce personal use (or abuse) of the Internet during business hours, while avoiding the administrative headaches of having to limit access.

My response was to simply deploy workstations in centralized locations throughout the building dedicated exclusively for the purpose of utilizing unlimited Internet access. Deny any Internet access to all other workstations, except those in the IT department of course. It's a near-perfect solution. Users can't download potential infected files, and since everyone knows who's on the Internet only workstation, users are far less likely to conduct personal business on company time. Turns out, the concept was reasonably successful. Just had to educate users on how to move files between workstations.

One of dumbest calls I think I've ever received was from a marketing director/wannabe IT Manager asking "How can I totally 100% secure our corporate network from the outside (meaning the Internet) to prevent unauthorized access?". How she managed to get involved with such a concept, I'll never know. My answer was "unplug the network from the Internet" and definitely was not appreciated.

Interpreter, Ambassador, and Diplomat

These are all titles which could easily describe your position as a Help Desk Technician interacting between the customer and your technical staff, most notably the programming department. I'm really referring to the ability to "Think Like a User". Since you are on the frontlines, you already know the value of being able to think like a user. It's often critical when troubleshooting a problem at the user's end. However, what I've experienced is the serious lack of the ability to think like a user particularly by those in the programming department. This is why I associate a Help Desk Tech to an Interpreter. You are able to translate the issue the user is having to the programming department in an effort to resolve the issue. You assuming the role as an ambassador refers to the relationship between you and the user.

And you being the diplomat means you're probably walking on eggshells every time you have to deal with the programming department.

Programmers most often don't think like a user. Because they don't user their own applications eight hours a day, five days a week, and therefore don't experience a lot of the little frustrating nuances the user must deal with. They are not likely to think about tab order on a busy data entry screen or making a procedural screen for importing a file more intuitive. Programmers usually don't realize most users don't think like programmers. The moral to this topic is if you're involved in applications design, be aggressive with your knowledge about what the user wants to see in an application. They're your bread and butter, your paycheck, and it will make you job less difficult.

Profanity

I bring this topic up even though those with limited common sense would already know never to use profanity in a professional environment. But one experience I had, really embraced the concept of never using profanity. This includes anything both written and verbal at the workplace. All it takes is a click of the mouse, and you've accidentally sent a profanity laced email, not to your best friend as part of humorous correspondence, but instead to your worst nightmare of a user.

The event I referred to occurred once when I was a manager of product support. I had a couple of employees, working their way through college, who had been hired as part time programmers. One of my responsibilities was to QA their work prior to releasing any updates to the customers.

An updated custom program released to a specific customer crashed, and as luck would have it, a whole bunch of comments in the source code containing obscenities directed at this particular customer appeared on her screen. Needless to say, the dirt hit the fan, and I caught most of the flack. It was about that time in my career I realized part of my job included both baby sitter and traffic cop. To this day, I don't understand how comments in source code could possibly be made visible at runtime.

Quality Control

There are few things I can think of in a place of business that peeves me off more than the guy who doesn't check his work before handing it back to me. One classic example is the programmer who applies a "fix", recompiles, and declares the problem solved – without even making sure the compiled application launches without error, not to mention checking it against the test case I spent a hours setting up so he wouldn't have to.

Another example is the DBA who gives me a first pass data conversion and asks me to take a look. Usually, within seconds, I can see that none of the countries where pulled over, leading zeros from zip codes have been dropped, or some other really obvious data error. All he had to do was take a minute or two and take a look himself. This would save considerable time for both of us. I've gone to the boss to complain about this, after all, time is money and the boss doesn't like to pay for wasted time. I have actually known "programmers" who, once a source compiled without syntax errors, considered the application bug free and available for general release. One gentleman's solution to an out-of-bounds array problem was to simply make the array larger. ID-10-T.

Nowhere else to put this little gem: A software vendor I was employed by decided to build in several hundred user requested enhancements into the flagship product that had been cumulating for a couple of years. There was nothing wrong with this, it was perfect timing as there had not been a previous major upgrade of the product for several years. The problem was they decided to just make thousands of code changes to the existing version without at least backing up all of the projects first and relocating to a different drive. So, for about a year the current release version could not be supported due to all of the code changes in progress without having to essentially debug both versions simultaneously. And, there were major changes in the database design as well.

The morel to this story is to make a "rubber stamp" copy of the version you are going to upgrade. Freeze the existing version, and unless there is some critical bug that needs to be addressed, leave it alone.

Reinventing the Wheel

An excellent example of SNAFU, after about six months attempting to write a CRM in one of the popular relational database apps at the time, the CUSTOMER SERVICE STAFF (naturally with absolutely no prior training in algorithm development whatsoever) was unable to deliver any semblance of a working CRM application. This a is classic case of a corporate entity trying to save big money by writing their own application from scratch, one which is already commercially available for a fraction of the cost. They spent 1 ½ man years, three employees for six months, and failed. I figure about $60,000 (1987) in paid salary for development vs. maybe $1,000 for the purchase of the application ready to go. And, that doesn't include the unanticipated cost of debugging and adding options they would have initially over looked. Amazing!

Yet I have seen this in every commercial niche market I've been involved with. I rescued the project by importing their data into a well known DOS CRM application and took me less than a day to complete. Problem solved.

Securing Networks

I had a customer call me one time to ask what the best solution is for securing a corporate LAN from digital intrusion. I explained there are firewalls, antivirus applications, and a variety of other security measures and methods that can be deployed. I further explained that all issues regarding network security issues should be the responsibility of the IT department. But this inquiry came from a small firm that didn't have an in-house IT department. She was fully aware that outsourcing this task was going to cost her a big chunk of budget. So the real purpose of her inquiry was really "how can I achieve the perfect solution to protect our network for free?". People only want to be told what they want to hear.

Version control, Tracking Software

Version control is nothing more than someone making a decision to "freeze" development on an application at a certain point based on some criteria. Freezing an application from additional change allows further development without having to be concerned about introducing bugs into a production version. The frozen version retains its' current version (or build) number, while the evolving application is assigned the next version number or build. Good documentation will help manage what has been implemented in what version, and can assist with reviewing software corrections historically.

Ultimately, tracking software is only as good as who participates. Naturally, the boss wants everything to be tracked – but in the end, it's always the boss who refuses to actually use it. The same can be said for contact management applications. Sales staff always seem to complain about having to manually enter names and addresses. Well, even so, if the current system isn't working, I guarantee a new, $20,000 cloud based application isn't going to work either. They all require the basic entry of data.

The boss also wants reports on various statues of support tickets. In a perfect world all of this stuff would be nice to have – if everybody participates and more importantly, everyone is allotted the time to maintain such systems. To the boss: you can't have your cake and eat it too. You're paying a staff to support your customers, you can't expect your staff to provide the same high level of support in addition to maintaining complex tracking systems.

I have some experience with tracking systems. Every one I've used was never up to date. Some had thousands of "open" tickets, others just had vague descriptions of reported problems. None had specific references to software corrections or delivery thereof. As I've mentioned on several occasions, my experience has been primarily with small shops. So, instead of expensive, time consuming tracking systems for bugs, I devised a simple paper system. Upon reproducing the bug in a test case, I print the appropriate number of screen shots (as many as it takes to describe the problem and how to cause it to fail) and staple a copy of the original email from the user. A few hand written notes briefly detailing the screen shots and perhaps rewriting the problem as the user described in their email, and I have a "ticket". The ticket is submitted to the programming department and return back to me upon correction.

If the test on the correction fails, the ticket goes back to the programming department. I recommend this simple system for larger shops, however, I would consider digitizing everything and maintaining a tracking folder on the network. Tickets, or files and folders, could be named using the date and 2 or 3 digit code depending on the volume of tickets. Thus ticket number 22 reported on January 11, 2011 would be assigned the tracking number 20110111022. It's really convenient to be able to pull a closed ticket for the same problem that has risen its' ugly head again.

Chapter 17 Uninterruptible Power Supplies (UPS)

Most of us have experienced that sickening feeling of dread when the power to our computer suddenly fails. Perhaps you had been working on that important month-end spreadsheet and hadn't saved your work (never depend on "auto-save" features), or your computer had been in the middle of your general ledger accounting applications' month-end close when suddenly the lights go out. It is at these moments when you wish you had an Uninterruptible Power Supply (UPS). Also known as a battery back-up, a UPS is basically a charged battery that delivers enough power to your computer to prevent it from immediately shutting down should the primary power source fail, such as in a blackout or brownout. In addition, the unit protects the computer and other connected devices from power surges and fluctuations that travel along your utility lines. UPS units come in different sizes and capacities depending on the computers' power requirements and the number of devices and peripherals.

Do You Need a UPS?

Unless you don't mind the risk of losing your most current data and having to restore from your last backup, the answer is "Yes." Your data is likely the life-blood of your business, and to operate without the protection a UPS exposes your data to possible corruption or complete loss, resulting in lost time, effort, and costs associated with restoring files from backup. If you are part of a network and your data files reside on a file server, it is very likely that the server already has a UPS in place. However, it is still recommended a UPS is deployed for each workstation.

Determining the Proper Capacity

As I previously mentioned, UPS systems come in different sizes and capacities. It is important to select the proper capacity for your particular situation. At the websites of most UPS manufacturers, you can follow a step-by-step process of selecting the right unit for your needs. The first step is to identify the general type of computer equipment to be protected. This means a single home or office workstation, or perhaps multiple network servers. Next, provide information about your computer's configuration including type (desktop, tower, etc.), monitor size, processor, number and types of internal hard drives, printers and other peripherals. Finally, specify how much run time to allow for a "soft" shutdown should power to your computer fail. Run times are generally from 5 to 60 minutes. Based on these parameters, the manufacturer will recommend UPS units appropriate for the amount of protection required.

Connecting the UPS to your Computer

Connecting your computer and peripherals to the UPS is simply a matter of plugging the power cords into the available outlets. Be aware though that some UPS units have a limited number of outlets that actually provide battery back-up. The remaining outlets only offer surge protection. So it is important your plug the main power cords for the computer, monitor and other important devices, such as an external hard drive, into these outlets. You can connect non-critical devices such as a printer or scanner into the secondary outlets.

Note: Plugging a UPS into itself does not, in fact, power your computer or other peripherals (Seriously, I have seen it tried!).

Most modern UPS units are equipped with a USB cable connected to your computer. This cable, along with supplied software, allows the UPS to communicate with your computer, reporting battery charge level, overall battery condition and other vital statistics. More importantly, the software monitors the power level to the UPS unit and should the power fail or drop below a certain level, it can automatically initiate a safe shut down of your computer. Most UPS units will also perform self-tests and will alert you to the results upon completion of the self-test, including when it's time to replace the battery.

What to Expect in a Power Outage

You are happily working on your computer when you see the lights and equipment around you suddenly dim. Since your computer is connected to the UPS, you will first hear an audible alarm. Despite the outage, your computer and other devices continue to operate normally. As you wait to see if the power is quickly restored, the alarm will continue. If it appears that the power is not returning immediately, you calmly save all your open documents, finish entering the last subscription order, and sign out of any other applications. Now, you initiate a normal shutdown of your computer. Once you confirm the computer has turned off, you should turn off the power to the monitor and all external hard drives and devices. Unfortunately, the audible alarm will continue but you can feel confident that your computer and the data that it manages are safe. What if you are not present at your computer when the power fails? The monitoring software provided by the UPS manufacturer will automatically initiate the shutdown procedure to your computer after a specific period of time.

Note: The possibility or power failures is another good reason never to leave open any applications or documents while your workstation is unattended for an extended length of time.

Embarrassing Story

Here's one that bit me in the backside. The battery for the UPS on one of my servers died, so I "borrowed" one from a workstation for temporary protection until the replacement battery arrived. The one I borrowed was a much smaller unit with only six outlets, three on a side. I didn't notice that three outlets on one side were actually protected exclusively by the battery. The three outlets on the other side were "straight through" and, although protected by the battery, were meant as a serge protector in the event the battery failed. And, it did the very next day. I had plugged in a couple of servers, a monitor, and the firewall randomly, figuring it wouldn't matter. Turns out one of the power cords was for the redundant power supply for the primary server and was plugged into the side that was not straight through. After researching what one of the indicator lights on the front panel of the server meant, I determined that one of the power supplies had failed. Only after installing a replacement power supply did I discovered my mistake. The morel to this embarrassing story is to take the time to read the specs. By the way, what's the best way to test a new or repaired UPS? Answer: make sure ever one's off the equipment protected by the UPS and unplug the UPS from the wall socket.

Conclusion

Your computers are under constant threat from viruses and 'malware', to hardware failure and operating system defects, and hopefully you have defenses and procedures in place to safeguard against these threats.

Protecting vital personal and corporate data from power outages and other power related threats can be mitigated by the use of a UPS. The cost and complexity of these units are nominal compared to what is at risk to you and your organization. If you are not already using a battery back-up device, drop what you are doing and get busy ordering one now!

Chapter 18 Backup and Restore

In any digital environment, home or office, absolutely nothing annoys me more than to find out there is no adequate procedure in place for backing up data. I had one case where a client called and wanted me to restore their data as their only computer had been stolen. Because I was the software vendor, they assumed I also somehow archived their data for them. I had the unfortunate task of explaining that I was in the business of providing software applications, of which I would be delighted to replace. They held me responsible for their loss, and I lost a paying customer. Other situations involved not having more recent backups which resulted in extensive rebuilding of databases. I know it's not your responsibility to babysit or play traffic cop, but losing a paid customer does hurt you. All I am suggesting is to take every opportunity to review current backup procedures with your customers.

Very rarely, data backups are necessary for purposes of restoration due to some type of failure, or catastrophic event. A broken cooling fan or a clogged air vent overheating a hard drive, a server restart without advance warning, or unscheduled maintenance by a technician can cause damage to specific files that may have been open at the time. For these unforeseen events, performing a complete backup of data on at least a weekly basis is highly recommended. More frequent backups are even better. An established schedule for rotation of backup media, and an off-site storage location for backup media are also highly recommended. Off-site rotation insures that your data is protected in the event of severe physical damage to the servers and/or workstations.

The selection of the media used to store the backup is crucial. I use shelf life as a guide to choosing what media I want to use for my backups. Archive grade DVD's tend to have a greater shelf life than tape cartridges and are relatively sturdy. I don't recommend re-recording over DVD's used for backups because I haven't found reliable information as to issues pertaining to reliability. The cost of a DVD doesn't justify trying to reuse DVD's. It's like trying to reuse generic sandwich baggies. Tape cartridges are good for about 250 rewrites, about five years based on my recommended rotation schedule. Tapes, CD's, and DVD's are all reasonably reliable, although I have experienced problems from time to time trying to recover data from them. Although removable hard drives are more reliable, removable hard drives are not as compact, and if a removable hard drive is dropped, chances are your data is gone. I recommend tape cartridge backups with DVD's as a supplement. I can easily pop a DVD into the mail to Grandma's house once a week insuring a reliable off-site rotated backup that can be read by virtually any PC.

My general rule for deciding a frequency and schedule for backup is "how much time can be afforded to re-enter all data for the period of time that has elapsed since the last backup?" Not only loss of time re-entering is a factor, but consider the margin for error anytime data must be manually entered.

The following is an example of a schedule for data backup and off-site rotation assuming you have a tape backup system with eight tape cartridges (each cartridge has the capacity to store one complete data backup), and that a complete backup is performed once a week:

Label the cartridges Weekly 1, Weekly 2, Weekly 3, Weekly 4, Quarterly 1, Quarterly 2, Quarterly 3, and Quarterly 4.

The first weekly backup begins with the cartridge labeled Weekly 1, the second week will use the cartridge marked Weekly 2, and so on. Week number five will use the cartridge marked Weekly 1, week number 6 will use the cartridge marked Weekly 2, and so on. The end of each quarter has its own backup set, the first quarter uses the cartridge marked Quarterly 1, the second quarter uses the cartridge marked Quarterly 2. It is recommended that the quarterly backups be rotated off-site.

I recommend complete backups as opposed to incremental backups. The latter is a current backup of only those files which have changed since the last backup. The advantage to an incremental backup is that it generally takes less time and storage capacity. The overwhelming disadvantage is the administrative nightmare to glue everything back together in the event you must restore from an incremental. And, if just one incremental restore fails, then you must go back to the last full backup, and that could easily translate into months of lost data.

Backed up data should be validated periodically by restoring. The restore can be selective, restore enough data to determine the backup media is valid. Make sure that you are able to read backup media off-site. I suggest all mission critical applications be installed on an offsite workstation. Backups can easily be verified by restoring data to the offsite workstation, then launching each mission critical application long enough to confirm the backup is successful and contains the most recent activity.

Consider a worst case scenario; your building has burned to the ground (I have had this happen, the customer lost everything, and their only backup was a removable hard drive which had been last updated almost a year prior to losing everything).

All of the servers, workstations, tape backup systems, removable hard drives, CD's, DVD's are all ash. What do you have offsite to restore your data? Assuming you have replaced your hardware, and if you have followed my guide, it takes only as long to restore your backup as it took to create the backup in the first place.

Red Tag

An example of the importance of offsite backups came to light in January of 1994. Many large office buildings were "red tagged" after the Northridge earthquake hit the greater Los Angeles area. Once a building is red tagged, no one is allowed in to recover anything. I know of several doctors who lost all of their data because they left their laptops in their offices and had no offsite backups.

Fire Proof Safes

I know first hand of an unfortunate incident whereby a gentlemen's house had burned to the ground in the infamous Malibu, California fire of 1993. He had stored his valuables, important papers, and digital media in his fire proof safe. He was finally able to go back to what was left of his home after the fire had been out for several days. Even though his fire proof safe was still hot from the fire, he opened the door. The instant the door was opened, all of the paper and digital contents vaporized. I don't profess to understand the thermal dynamics of exactly what happened, but simply put, the safe was hot and its' contents were in a vacuum. When the door was opened, much cooler air was allowed in. So much for fire proof safes.

Cloud Services

Offsite backups to Internet data warehouses, also known as "Cloud" services are becoming more popular. However, it is important to note a few things before committing all of your valuable data:

1) Charges are usually by the gigabyte, and costs can add up if your file management leaves anything to be desired.

2) Keep in mind that your data is no longer under your exclusive control. Although highly unlikely, it does mean that your data exists in another physical location and could be compromised.

3) Should you require restoration of all or part of your data, be prepared to wait for perhaps as much as 24 hours while the Cloud service builds your restore job for downloading. Then allow perhaps hours to download your data (how long did it take to upload initially?).

4) Consider the time and resources necessary to upload your data from your network to the Cloud service. Backups should be scheduled during off hours.

5) One advantage to using a Cloud service for backing up data is that incremental backups do make sense. Even though you are backing up only what has changed since the last backup, you do have a complete set of backed up data in one physical location.

6) You should also evaluate backup retention for complete (not incremental) backup sets (how long will your backup for a specific date remain available) for purposes of restoration. If you discover a file is corrupted and it has since been backed up, then you will need to access yet an earlier backup.

If the service maintains files going back only 30 days and you need something from two months ago, the service is obviously not going to work in that case.

In summary, even if your data is securely stored in a Cloud, other factors can prohibit access to your data. Network outages (either your end, or on the service providers' end, or both) , denial of service attacks against the service provider, any failure of the service providers' infrastructure, or the service provider simply goes out of business, are all unlikely but possible events.

Paper is Going to be Around a Long Time

I have pulled people off of paper systems to digital environments, as recent as about 2005. I still print emails and screen shots just because they're easier to read after staring at a monitor all day. Plus I use paper as a method of tracking bug fixes. When a bug gets fixed, I staple all of the programmer's notes, my notes, and the bosses' notes in one neat bundle for the filing cabinet. I don't know of an efficient method of backing up paper, so in the event of fire or flood you'll lose your paper. But that's why programmers are supposed to add comments in the source code, and if everyone cooperated on the use of a tracking system (I discuss this elsewhere), there would little need for paper, even for me.

Other than my simple method for tracking problems, hand written annotations on draft documentation and white boards are the only other exceptions. But if you must drop a note to a coworker or your boss, be sure to write clearly and use the same rules for spelling and grammar as though it was your own resume.

I find it irritating when "Bill" sticks his head in my office and asks my why Mr. Brown's phone number (scrawled on a scrap of paper and taped to Bill's monitor by the department manager) was for a company located in San Francisco. Upon closer examination of the scrap of paper, I noticed the date "4 15 ", was ominously close to what appeared to be a phone number. I later mentioned to the department head that he should have been a doctor. Had the phone number been emailed or IM'd, I wouldn't have wasted twenty minutes of my time tracking down a phone number, not to mention the considerable annoyance of the interruption in the first place.

Chapter 19 Viruses, Malware, and Spyware

For all of you experts who fix this stuff for a living, I realize this is basic material. My goal here is to review this topic with the intention of creating awareness for novice techs. The potential for catastrophic damage is on the same level as not having backed your data. Should you get infected by a particularly vicious brand of malware, be prepared to spend considerable time and money to get rid of it. If you let it go very long, you risk propagation of the attack to the point where your backups become infected and are rendered completely useless. This chapter on viruses, malware, and spyware applies primarily to those of you who support in-house users. Depending on the specific problems that arise when supporting users remotely, advising users to run scans periodically should be an integral part of your support procedure.

Computer malware, also known as malicious software, by definition can include viruses, but often differ from viruses in that malware is usually harmful with the intent of achieving financial gains by illegal means. Malware, like viruses, can "reproduce", or attach themselves to other files allowing for propagation throughout entire networks, and indeed, throughout the World Wide Web. Destruction to operating systems and files differ depending on the threat level of the malware or virus. Spyware is a type of malware that attempts to retrieve data, such as websites visited, financial information, and even series of keystrokes (which could contain usernames and passwords).

Unfortunately, there is no inexpensive solution to implementing a reasonable level of protection from malware, virus, and spyware attacks particularly on the corporate level.

There are a few shareware, or "free", apps available, but these are intended for personal use, and unless you are willing to be patient with the advertising pop-ups that arrive with shareware, it's not a solution for doing business in a professional environment. And, beware, many "shareware" applications claim to protect against these attacks when in reality they are actually malware apps themselves (these are referred to as "ransom ware").

My first and only experience with a virus attack in a professional environment was in early 2001 when the Kournikova virus prolithereated around the world causing untold hundreds of millions of dollars in digital destruction, including the network which I was an administrator. I spent dozens of hours repairing, and in some cases, a total wipe and reinstall of all the infected workstations. On the bright side this experience served as a wakeup call, I immediately ordered the corporate enterprise version of one of the most popular antivirus applications at the time. There was significant upfront cost and management wasn't happy about it. But after evaluating the resources spent on repairing the Kournikova attack, it became clear the cost was easily justified. Since the Kournikova attack, I have remained vigilant about monitoring and maintaining all anti-virus, anti-malware, and anti-spyware. The priority for this type of threat prevention should be second only to your backup procedures and other network security functions. As of this writing, I have not had a single event of contamination within a corporate LAN where I was an administrator.

However, PC's at home are a different story. Because my extended family and friends know what I do for a living, well, anytime they have a computer problem I get the call.

Usually, the repair amounts to just deleting temporary Internet files and running a scan from whatever anti-virus app that happens to be installed. But, once in awhile I get a workstation on which there has never been any protection.

One experience I had was a malware infected PC. None of the descriptions I was able to find for that particular malware app mentioned any particular threat level or what type of destruction it was capable of, but I found out soon enough. That particular malware app would not let any programs launch, so I was unable to install anything to get rid of it. It would not let me boot in Safe Mode, and it would not let me boot from a CD. It wouldn't let me into CMD. I wasn't even able to get to the infected hard drive with a bootable floppy (and yes, I have a USB 3 ½ inch floppy drive, some of these malware apps can be defeated because they forgot to disable the floppy drive). Since the data on the infected hard drive had never been backed up, my game plan got a whole lot more complex. I bought an identical hard drive, installed it into the infected PC, and installed the OS and the anti-virus/anti-malware apps. I disconnected the infected hard drive during that process. Once I had an operational system, I reconnected the infected hard drive as a slave and ran the anti-virus and anti-malware apps. I then safely backed up all of the data from the infected drive to the new drive.

I disconnected the new drive and was now able to boot the previously infected drive. However, although you could navigate, view pictures, and launch some of the installed apps, the previously infected drive was unable to perform most of the system related functions one would find in a control panel. So, one last step – run the recovery tool.

Accessing the recovery tool differs on across various makes and models.

In this case, holding down Alt and tapping F10 during the initial boot did the trick. Now all I had to do was figure out the password: someone's cats' name.

Ok, got the password and am starting to recover. And while I'm here and it's prompting me, I might as well go ahead a burn a recovery CD. Because, if you lose the recovery partition, you're in a brand new world of hurt. Remember the recovery tool will usually overwrite the installed OS, and you will lose your data. Back your data up before running any recovery tool or procedure. I recommend running one industry standard antivirus app for all of your antivirus and malware requirements. Running multiple antivirus apps can cause severe performance degradation and in some cases, other applications and printers will fail.

Industry standard protection applications are highly recommended along with maintaining annual subscriptions to all application updates and virus and malware definitions. Be vigilant for any news of new outbreaks and make sure your virus definitions are always up to date. For corporate networks, go with the complete enterprise editions of anti-malware and anti-virus apps. Second to a robust backup procedure, it's the best insurance you'll ever purchase.

Tip: On all machines, home or professional, workstation or server, always set up a couple of additional administrative users. If one of the administrative profiles gets infected, you have the other administrative users available to remove the malware (assuming the malware only infects that profile). It's an extra layer of protection which has saved me a tremendous amount of extra work.

Chapter 20 Air Conditioning and Bathroom Wars

How familiar does this sound? Constantly fighting to keep office areas cool to help prevent computer failures just doesn't seem to make any sense to staff or co-workers. The ladies are always complaining about how cold it is, yet they're wearing low-cut sleeveless blouses and miniskirts. You can always put on another sweater, legally, you can only take so much off. I actually had one wing nut threaten to call SECURITY on me for not letting the little baby turn on the heat. Mind you, this was a Saturday morning, I was a MANAGER, and he was just an entry level programmer. I won.

Allowing access to a thermostat to anyone in the office is a huge mistake. Undoubtedly, most everyone will adjust it to their own liking. This not only causes extreme wear and tear on the heating and a/c equipment, it can shut it down completely. In one office, they kept the heat and a/c adjustments pinned next to each other causing heat and a/c to cycle back and forth. The a/c just froze over and quite working.

If you work at a small company like I have most of my career, then you are probably relegated the task of refilling the restroom TP, soap etc. Now, I don't mind this, but it's when the boss "forgets" to order soap, air freshener, TP, etc. Well, the easy solution (if you don't want to confront directly), is when it runs out, replace with the most revolting air freshener, harshest soap (I recommend that brand that comes from a volcano), and about the equivalent to no. 3 sandpaper for the TP. That should get the job done.

Chapter 21 The Help Desk Tech as an Employee

Beyond the scope of a Help Desk Tech's official daily duties, there are other areas of importance which I would like to share. In this chapter, I am emphasizing job security and how to maintain it, along with a few other suggestions. At the time of this writing, the economy appears to be headed for a recovery from the worst recession in seventy-some years. A lot of folks have learned the hard way about being too complacent with their job, not keeping their job (computer) skills up to date, and not increasing their overall value to their employer. However, regardless of your skill level, job performance, salary, or seniority, never forget that you are always expendable. Employers often make bad personnel decisions and they don't have to justify themselves.

Documentation

I actually enjoy documenting. Whether it is user's guides, websites, or just proofing the boss' newsletter, it can be very rewarding. Your Help Desk Technical position gives you a distinct advantage in that you are more knowledgeable about the products you support and your corporate infrastructure. Remember, one of my key elements to achieving success in your position and to maintain job stability is to Make Yourself as Valuable as possible. I have found that writing and maintaining FAQ's and Knowledge Base articles are powerful tools for enhancing Help Desk and support functions (I make it clear to users that these tools are only meant to supplement the Help Desk, not replace it).

Make available easy to read single paragraph FAQ's and KB Articles either by emailing links to your website or by simply attaching the article to an email thus increasing response time to your users.

One of the advantages of documenting which works for me is by having to key something into a temporary file (perhaps adding to an article later) helps me remember that information for later use. As far as I'm concerned, documents are useless unless spelling, punctuation, and grammar are correct. This is especially true for web sites. I have witnessed blatant errors on even the home page of a corporate web site resulting in lost sales. Prospective clients viewing your web site with errors in spelling and grammar aren't going to take long to wonder about what the products are like. There's really no excuse for spelling errors since word processors do a pretty good job of spell checking. Misspelled words and bad grammar equate to laziness. You don't get a second chance to make a good first impression.

And, by the way, how much information, and what kind of information, should be published on your companies' web site? Knowing your competitors can also view your website, I suggest limiting Knowledge Base articles and FAQ's to productive topics with a marketing theme. You don't need to broadcast to the competition or prospective clients about all of the wonderful workarounds your company provides due to limitations or issues with your applications. Also, too much information allows users who do not subscribe to a support contract resolve issues on their own when they otherwise might be renewing their contract. Never put any documentation online, especially descriptions of file formats and layouts, even if it has a copyright.

As long as we're on the subject, due diligence must be exercised on all company trademarks, patents, and copyrights to ensure they remain the property of the company. Failure to protect such property, regardless of reason, may jeopardize such protection and materials become public domain.

Education Never Ends

Only you are accountable for staying current with changes in technology. Unless you are directed to perform research and development on company time, staying on top of your profession is your responsibility, on your time. I know, for example, many folks employed in the medical profession must attend seminars at their own expense just to keep their license to practice current. I explain this concept to users when they complain about not being able to navigate through new versions of operating systems and other applications. I always take the opportunity to suggest courses related to upgrading computer skills at a local community college or other institution to users I feel won't be offended. Users too lazy to keep themselves updated on even the most trivial issues will instead try to take advantage of your resources. In other words, they want you to educate them on topics outside of the scope of your support responsibility.

The same concept applies when hiring new staff. I was both amazed and amused at a comment one of my old supervisors once made. After the second person he had hired in as many years quit as his assistant, he exclaimed "I can't believe I got suckered again for a paid education!". Of course there are really two issues here, he's right about the paid education, but on the other hand he's the one who hired them.

He lacked the ability to find someone with the right blend of common sense and experience while attempting to stay within an unrealistic hiring budget. I was the one he was trying to replace as I had been promoted elsewhere within the company.

Firing

Been down this road too. If you have the authority to hire, then you likely have the authority to let someone go. Be prepared for total emotional breakdown when you let someone go.

Going Down With the Ship

As long as we're on the subject of layoffs, here's looking at it from a different perspective:

Hmmm, you've just gotten out of a meeting with the big boss and several other mangers and leading staff members. The topic: How can we increase revenue? (Isn't that his job?)

That's an interesting question especially if you are a small niche software provider which specializes in a particular industry. Odds are, revenue is generated from your core product, add-on's (or modules), subscription support, and custom software development. It's an interesting question because it sends up one whopper of a red flag. I've experienced these kinds of meetings on several occasions throughout my career, and they mean only one thing: things aren't going very well and it's probably time to update your resume and turn the heat up on you social looking-for-a-job networking skills.

Meanwhile, you'll probably have to ride out the storm. From a support standpoint, I've satisfied such questions from the big boss by offering ideas to bundle "value added" services. For example, call it a 10,000 mile checkup. For $299.00, a Technical Support staff member will review the customers' folder and file structure and perform any "housecleaning" (under the guise this will boost system performance), and organizing.

Offer free training to encourage customers to renew their subscription maintenance. Or, build that custom report they've been asking for the past year – at no charge. Update the documentation and make a special announcement by email blast that it's available to all active subscribers of subscription support. Publish your newsletter monthly instead of quarterly (for awhile), and offer legitimate "how-to's" not just on your applications, but on applications that yours might be used in conjunction with. Emailing announcements and newsletters are more likely to get the attention of your customer base because they simply aren't going to take the time to visit your web site.

These are just a few things I've come up with. Perhaps you can think of other value-added incentives. Be creative, look at things from where your customer sits. You should know because you are the eyes and ears of your organization, your customer base, and the industry you serve.

Hiring

While I suppose there is prestige for those who have the authority to hire staff, you can bet their butt's are going to be called on the carpet if a hire goes south. A lot of explaining at very least. Put simply, there is significant cost involved particularly when a recent hire doesn't pan out. I know, I've been down that road. And I don't want to be called on the carpet.

Job Complacency, Make Yourself Valuable

From an employee standpoint, cross training *should* apply to everyone (except TS'ers, who don't believe in ever being complacent with any employment situation). From management's point of view, cross training *does* apply to everyone.

Cross training isn't new, there is just more awareness. Wearing a few more hats is more accepted (although not necessarily popular) as a necessity, especially during these past couple of years due to economic conditions. Turn this challenge into a positive thing by adding your new skills to your resume. If you're not assigned anything specific, then look for a few things to increase your value by increasing the value of what you are responsible for. If you see something that needs to be done, and you are qualified, do it without waiting to be told. Even the little things, such as keeping the paper trays loaded, cleaning the coffee pot, topping off the soap dispenser, wiping down the microwave, and cleaning the fridge will get the boss' attention eventually.

At one employer, I was the senior help desk tech. But I also doubled as the network administrator, and assumed the task of maintaining system backups. I took over updating the User's Guides for our flagship products and became the senior proof reader for all marketing materials. As the assistant to the MIS at another organization, I was able to perform all my tasks efficiently enough to spend time in the repair department. I not only perfected my soldering and de-soldering skills, I learned quite a lot about warehousing and inventory control. This in turn was an unexpected bonus as I later went on to support an inventory application.

Once, I had a printer with part of the feeder failing. It was a rubber roller that guided the sheet to the output tray that had worn out. I was a new employee at the time, and I expected to be told to send the printer out for repair. Surprisingly, I was told instead to find the part, order it, and replace it. And, it worked! From that time on, I always attempt repairs on my own. Incidentally, I also replaced a cooling fan in one the workstations that had failed.

That was a fun little project, and it gave me a chance to brush up on my soldering skills (it just so happened the company I worked for at the time is a distributor for a leading brand of solder equipment). This experience also taught me the value of saving old machines for purposes of parting them out.

Yet another duty I once assumed was managing the proximity locks in the building. Programming entry badges for new and terminated employees, replacing battery packs, and keeping the mechanism lubricated was all part of this particular job. Naturally, as things go, I ended up being the lube guy for all of the doors in the facility. Note: I used silicon lubricant specifically for all door and lock mechanisms, not the stuff that just repels water.

I play on my strengths, one of which is a jack-of-all-trades. I have finite knowledge about a wide variety of subjects, but I do not specialize in any particular area. This allows me a greater level of comfort when I have to research a subject in detail.

Justifying Your Role

At one of the positions I held as a help desk tech, I was hired because, in addition to my qualifications, my predecessor wasn't working out. I never asked any questions about the situation, but it was obviously not an amicable departure. (Never get involved with this type of history within the company. It is an embarrassment to the boss, and he's not going to be happy discussing it with anybody, least of all you). The history of this particular individual became evident anyway, because I inherited his workstation, profile (with Internet Favorites and browsing history), email, all of his personal files, and quite a vast collection of games.

You can figure out from what I just described why he didn't last very long. But what got me was the email correspondence with the users he was supposed to support. If he did manage to offer an answer to a customers' inquiry, it often took days, or even weeks before the user was provided a response. Most of the time, email from users with bugs, questions, or other issues was simply forwarded on to one of the programmers. There was no effort made to compile a list of answers to questions that should have been posed to the user, never any test cases to try to reproduce the problem for the programmer, or any attempt to arrive at a workaround for the user in the meantime. He never justified his role.

Lay Offs

Ever watched one of those old war submarine movies? Where one guy is on the other side of the sealed hatch drowning, knowing he's bought the farm and the other guy watches knowing he is going to be okay? Well, on more than one occasion that's how I felt knowing a key guy just got his walking papers. What can you do? I can tell you what I did for whatever it's worth. I re-wrote his resume and cover letter for him, and put together a brief summary of a few things I pulled from this guide to prepare him for (hopefully) imminent interviews. The work paid off, he landed an interview the day after he submitted the resume and cover that I wrote for him. Getting an interview is a great shot of confidence. It means the prospective employer paid attention to his resume, and his qualifications for the position. Hopefully, I will have a happy ending to this story, we'll see what happens. The point here is, no matter the reason, and in this case a seasoned technical guy, had to start pounding pavement. Here's where you come in.

Offer yourself as a qualified reference. Review the strengths and, more importantly what to respond to as his weaknesses (I have covered these areas elsewhere in this guide). Emphasize that fact that it could just as easily have been you in his shoes, and perhaps, soon it will be. Let me further emphasize that I offer myself as a professional reference only in situations where I can clearly confirm the credentials of those to whom I have made this offer. You don't want to refer "dead wood" and then somehow down the road it bites you in the backside.

Line Up All Your Ducks

I make a game out of trying to anticipate what the boss' is really requesting when he gives me a side project. The bottom line is I always give him more than he asked for. An example might be "give me a cost breakdown on what the different postage rates are for sending a package containing two hard bound User's Guides and a set of CD's". Now I know he's asking specifically for United States Postal Service postage rates. What I give him is a spreadsheet with the dimensions and weight of each package along with the USPS rate, but I include rates for all of the major carriers, Federal Express, UPS, and a courier service just to round it out.

If he wants a history of a specific problem for a specific client, provide him with a detailed timeline of the event he is asking for. The source might be a problem tracking system, email history, or a paper file, but provide not only information on the specific problem, but anything that might be related. Related issues could include a history of hardware issues at the client site, personnel turnaround, or lack of effective training. Chances are, if he's asking you for this type of information on a client, there's something going on, and you don't want to risk being seen as "dropping the ball".

Pat-on-the-Back

You're in the business where almost all correspondence you receive will be problems. I have, on occasion, received both letters and emails of gratitude from customers. Actually, my boss received them and shared them with me. It's always nice to get a positive note once in awhile. Save all letters and emails of commendation as they help you build up credibility. If there is ever a dispute with a customer, the boss is far more likely to side with you.

Sales and Marketing

Whether you are a manager, supervisor, or member of the technical staff, you must never avoid any event that has a potential for income. Your involvement in both sales and marketing, whether the Senior VP of Sales or the Marketing Manager likes it or not, is critical to the future health of the company. Marketing of products and services containing false or misleading information or specifications (unintentional or otherwise) is going to make your life much more difficult. You will ultimately support the stuff that doesn't work, or doesn't exist. Stay informed, pay attention to sales pitches and sales promotions. You are often the first line of offense for the best potential customers there are – yours. Be prepared to market and sell your products to your customer base.

Stress and Your Health

I've been told on many occasions by my superiors supporting users requires some pretty "thick skin". This comment was meant to be a form of encouragement and support. Keeping the users and the bosses off your back (preferably happy as well) can be stressful.

Not everyone is suited to perform this kind of work, and most folks I've seen who were offered a role in support staff backed off obligingly. Nobody likes rejection and there's a lot of it in Help Desk and Technical Support roles.

I'm not qualified as a physician to offer any medical advice. But, I can tell you what I do to help ease stress from job-related events. One of the ways I combat job-related stress is by leaving technology behind as much and as often as I can. My cell phone is pay-as-you-go and I use it for outbound calls only. I don't know its' phone number, and have never answered it (not that anyone has called). I'm not a gamer, and I don't get on the computer at home except when it's work related or I need to take a look at my checking account (yes, I still write checks as opposed to handing out my account number to the utilities, cable company, and telephone company thus allowing them to dip into my account anytime they choose).

After a long day at the office, I take walks on some evenings and visit the Jacuzzi on others. I get a few things ready for work the next day, a little TV, after which I hit the hay. I get up early enough to turn on the TV and watch a little of the morning news. The key is to give myself enough time to prepare to leave for work at a casual pace. In fact, I've even changed the route I take on my commute. I'm fortunate the "Old Road" as it is now known, parallels the freeway for about half my commute. The old road was the major highway before the present Interstate was built many years ago. Even though my new commute adds a couple extra miles and maybe an extra ten minutes, it's literally a drive through the countryside. There is far less traffic, which translates to less stress for me, and I can sip on a cup of coffee as well.

My hobby is camping and my favorite weekend getaway is any one of the primitive areas of the Mojave Desert or Sierra Nevada Mountains in California. Lighter fluid, my BBQ, and my tent are the most advanced technologies I deal with on my outings. All of the music I require is provided by Mother Nature. I rarely even bring reading material. I spend the days doing a little hiking, the evenings enjoying a nice campfire and gazing at the night sky. Mental health is just as important as physical health, and I recommend taking regular breaks.

Telecommuting

Particularly in difficult economic times, when gaining employment is difficult and you want to stay employed, I suggest you nix the idea of working from home. It can become difficult for the one who signs your paycheck to realize your value if he can't physically see you. Plus, if you're not around, you risk losing control over the domain you've worked so hard to put in place.

Vacation

Studies by the medical field have shown that vacation plays an important role in the overall health of employees. I always take complete advantage of vacation time with a couple of exceptions; I typically don't take more than one full week at a time, and I do check in with the office a once or twice during the week. Yes, I know, this doesn't sound like a real vacation and I am not secure about completely leaving the office. Both true, but I have worked for small companies my entire career which means when I am gone, someone has to double duty. If I can help avoid a crisis in the office by taking 15 or 20 minutes a couple times during the week via phone (land line because I am out of cell range), then that is well spent time.

If you're managing staff whom you must communicate with on vacation anymore than I suggested above, then you shouldn't be managing staff in the first place. I don't manage based on the precise minute an employee arrives or departs from the office, I manage based on both quality and quantity of output. This applies more so to technical staff that don't have to abide by set office hours to provide technical support. Obviously, if your support contract states specific hours of operation for which your customers pay, then those hours must be enforced.

Are you appreciated upon your return from an extended vacation? An excellent barometer is determined by how much of a cluster pack waits for you once you get back. If everything runs smoothly during your absence, this is a good indication upper management won't be questioning the value of your position.

Work Ethics, Working From Home

As I briefly mentioned elsewhere in this guide, telecommuting can cost you control over what goes on in the office. If you're not there, other employees have a tendency to change, break, and disrupt procedures and work in progress which you have worked so hard to maintain. Lack of physical presence in the office can create the illusion interpreted by management that you are no longer of any value to the company.

However, I spent nearly ten years running my own business out of my home. Surprisingly, there were few interruptions or distractions that precluded me from being highly productive. I adapted well to that working environment, but I had to institute some rules with the rest of my family. For example, I established normal business hours. Just like most office environments, I was not to be disturbed with non-emergency personal matters during business hours.

This took a little time to sink in, and you have to be adamant and enforce the rules.

I also found I worked longer hours without the additional fatigue I get in a typical office situation. I can account for that simply by the lack of commuting. The fact that my paycheck depended on only me, with no one else to lean on, also helped with the motivational aspects of working out of the house.

You Really Want to be a Manager?

Frankly, all lot of times, being a manger just isn't worth the additional compensation. Take a look around at what managers are responsible for in your organization. Are they still in their office after you leave for the day? Is there any free space on their whiteboards to write ANYTHING? How many stacks of paper (and how high) are strewn about their office? And, how many "Masters of the Universe" do they have to answer to? When it involves support, guess who gets to deal with the most difficult of customers? Not to mention having to liaison with consultants, accountants, and virtually all areas within the firm.

Chapter 22 Resume Formats

I agree with the professional resume writers about most of the "rules" for writing a resume. And I've seen some whoppers. The first batch to get pitched, the easiest ones, are the ones the size of "War and Peace". I've had as many as fifteen pages of a single resume faxed to me. Anything over two pages gets filed in the circular. Those containing spelling or gross grammatical errors are the next batch to get tossed. Now it's down to content.

Resumes typically get less than ten seconds of attention before they are either pitched or set aside for further evaluation. Just imagine yourself as the manager responsible for a new hire having received hundreds of resumes out of which you must decide what to review in detail. Keywords such as "increased revenue", or "20% decrease in call volume" will boost the chances of your resume making it through digital filters that many potential employers use to evaluate resumes submitted online or via email.

I look primarily for accomplishments. You can't accomplish anything if you don't have the qualifications in the first place. How many man-hours did you save by deploying version tracking? How much money did you save your previous employers by streamlining their support functions, and how did you accomplish that? How much revenue did you generate? And yes, you're supposed to sell regardless of what your job description says (at very least, outstanding balances due for subscription support).

I like a single page resume (see Appendix C for my preferred resume format).

I like to see the first page begin with a few lines summarizing operating system environments and major applications the candidate has experience with. Followed by a summary of hardware platforms, obviously computers, but what about routers, switches, telephone systems, and even proximity locks? Employment dates going back ten years are usually sufficient, followed by formal education, a list of any publications, and finally any miscellaneous items such as citizenship status and security clearances.

By the way, I don't care what your "objective" is. I already know. It's to get a job. And, I really could care less whether the candidate plays bridge, basketball, or sits on his can watching TV in his free time. So don't waste my time, or yours, with stuff that doesn't have anything to do with the employment opportunity.

While the resume is somewhat generic, (although you should always fine tune it to the specific job description when possible) the cover letter should highlight accomplishments that are directly related to the job position. Do the research. Visit the prospective employers' website and learn about the business. You want to be able to demonstrate in the cover letter why you would be an excellent candidate for the position. If a website is not listed, look at the email address of the responder. See Appendix D for my preferred cover letter format.

I don't recommend including any personal information such as street address on resumes or cover letters that may get posted online.

You the Interviewee

A side from the obvious, appropriate attire and grooming, I recommend carrying a binder. One of those fake leather types that you can insert an 8 ½ by 11 writing pad on one side, and a place for several copies of your resume, cover letter, and references on the other side. And a couple of ball point pens. I have actually gone on a second interview where the interviewer lost my resume. The binder gives you a more professional look, and you have something to take notes with while keeping your hands busy.

Note: The fact that a potential employer lost your resume should send up a red flag for you. Not to mention all of the two foot high stacks of paperwork, magazines, and newspapers strewn about the office caused me to wonder about the organizational and time management skills of my potential employer. By the way, take a look at Appendix G where I have listed some job descriptions (I actually pulled these right off the boards) and my real world interpretation of what those descriptions might actually mean.

You already know that you will get grilled about your strengths, but have you ever thought about how to respond when asked about your weaknesses? I have one technique that not only provides an honest, and noteworthy answer, it actually turns the whole weakness thing into an advantage. My weakness is a tendency to give away (at no charge), sometimes maybe a little too much, to keep the customer happy. I am not talking about giving away the entire product line, or spending weeks on some development project for free. Depending on the magnitude of the crisis, I might give the zip code database at no charge. Or perhaps a minor module, something with one of the lowest price points of the product line. I might spend an hour showing a user how to export data from the product I support, import that data into a spreadsheet, and build a few formulas to arrive at the desired results. The company is not going to go broke, and you keeps another happy customer.

Qualifications for specific areas are important. I pay less attention to the guy who can paper his wall with diplomas and certificates, and more attention to those who have real world experience. My biggest peeve are those who never check their work before handing it to whoever's next in line – usually me. That includes customer service personnel who don't check corrections on sales orders, programmers who don't test their bug fixes on the test case that I spent two hours setting up for them in the first place, and the wing nut sales person that can't, or won't, use the spell checker on the letter he's about to send to his most important client.

Changing Jobs, Leaving the Company

A word of caution, often times the newbie is the first to get the ax. I have always made it a point not to get too greedy about salary. The Great Recession of 2009 taught me the higher salaried were the first to go, leaving entry level users to fill the gap. That's great if you are part of an organization that provides service. I'll never understand management which offs its best personnel, only to have to hire twice the number of lesser skilled replacements to accomplish the same productivity at an even greater expense.

It's important to realize when you quit, for all intents and purposes, you're firing your boss. Put into this perspective, I recommend departing as amicably as possible. Give at least the traditional two weeks notice, and write a letter of resignation thanking the management and staff for an enlightening eight years of challenges, blah, blah, blah. I go so far as offer my time after departure in the event there are any questions concerning where things are or how I resolved a particular issue, and so forth.

Burning bridges is never an option. You always want to keep all doors open because you never know what lies in the future. And, my advice includes any reason for leaving no matter how much your professional relationship has deteriorated.

Chapter 23 The New Building

This chapter is on the border of the scope of my original goal of providing a guide for basic technical support concepts. But if you ever have to physically relocate, there may be a thing or two here that might be of assistance. I've gone down this road a few times, moving a business is a giant pain in the back side. It's like moving every employee to a new house all at once.

On one of those occasions my employer bought a brand new building, the building was built to our specific design parameters, literally, from the ground up. I picked up quite a few tricks on this experience. The level of detail in planning this move was overwhelming. But in the end, 15,000 square feet of warehouse including equipment, furniture, computers, and inventory were completely moved over the course of a single weekend. We shutdown at our normal time on Friday, and were open for business three days later at 7:30am Monday morning without so much as a lost bolt. And that's what I will be describing in this chapter.

Each department was responsible for tagging their own equipment, furniture, and boxes, as well as making sure everything arrived intact at the correct location. Some departments had a lot more on their plate than others. The training facility, repair lab, and the warehouse had a far greater challenge than the administration or customer support departments. Interestingly, those who didn't really have anything to move managed to justify their role by, for all-intents-and-purposes, cutting out "paper dolls" (paper models of desks, tables, and filing cabinets), and spending hours arranging their new office. Incredibly, management overlooked this huge waste of time.

The new offices were all modular and most of the existing furniture was discarded. Perhaps the management intentionally intended to keep them out of everybody else's way.

As a member of the IT staff, my primary responsibility was the design of the data center for the new building. But, design also included the LAN infrastructure within the entire building, configuration of conduit for all of the electrical, phone systems, network cabling, and air conditioning and power requirements. And, if that wasn't enough, an accurate estimate of the company's growth had to be considered to allow for all future requirements for additional capacity before construction was completed.

One of the first tasks was to estimate the total power requirement for the building. I reviewed every piece of equipment which plugged into a wall socket, from the largest conveyor system down to the desk top calculators, and recorded the wattage. The total amount of power multiplied by the growth estimate of the company gave us a number for overall power requirements. Another estimate was calculated for essential equipment including servers, workstations, and phones for the battery backup system.

After seemingly endless hours in design meetings, I finally won the argument over what type of UPS would be deployed. I vigorously lobbied against a proposed gas-turbine engine powered generator that would have provided backup power for about a week. Although it most certainly would have been nice to have, it was simply too impractical. The overhead for maintenance and time and materials on such a system was going to be too expensive. Besides, if local infrastructure were going to be down more than a day for whatever catastrophic reason, we weren't going to be able to ship anything anyway.

Instead, I successfully argued for a battery backup system, the manufacturer of which is probably the most well known. The model of the UPS was basically a cabinet roughly the size of a VW van loaded with fifty or so "car" batteries.

Ultimately, this system was the optimal choice. Unfortunately, nobody listened to me when I recommended the UPS be ordered and installed BEFORE the building was completed. I actually had to take measurements of the cabinet and build a mockup out of refrigerator crates to see if we could get it up the stairwell (naturally, the computer room was on the second floor). The mockup proved the real cabinet would fit. It took six guys and a power dolly to get the cabinet moved to the proper location. And then, one by one, each of the fifty batteries was hauled upstairs for reinstallation back into the cabinet.

The Move

Moving was tightly scheduled. Obviously, everything had to be tagged with a destination. Office stuff was easy, it was the inventory in the warehouse (over 7,000 separately cataloged items) which had to be moved without losing a single piece. The moving company which was contracted to assist had to be constantly supervised by office and warehouse staff. I physically moved all of the IT hardware using a separately rented box truck.

Settling In

There were still many tasks that required completion. Right down to installing the orange face plates on the electrical outlets exclusively for the UPS. The theory was to have only mission critical hardware plugged into the UPS via an outlet with an orange face plate, thus conserving batteries in the event of a power failure.

183

I could never convince one wing nut that his paper shredder was not counted as mission critical.

I did have a procedure to follow in the event of a power failure, fortunately I only had to perform it a couple of times. As soon as power to the building failed, I physically toured the entire facility beginning at the back of the warehouse and worked my way to the front office, then the second floor administrative offices, finally to the computer room. Along the way I ordered all non-essential hardware to be powered off (remember, this is hardware plugged into the orange plated outlets that are on the UPS). For example, the warehouse was allowed one workstation to print picking tickets and shipping labels. Customer Service was allowed one workstation for data entry and printing of sales orders. The PDC, VoIP, and Print Server were required to remain up. This configuration would provide about nine hours, a full business day, of up time before the batteries were drained.

Incidentally, the default home page on my browser was the local power company. At the time, they enforced rolling blackouts in an emergency, but you could get a rough idea if you were going to get hit by checking the location code on your electric bill against the rolling blackout schedule on their web site.

We also had redundancy in the phone system. In the event of VoIP or T1 failure, we had several analog lines on a rotary. The Telco was directed to forward our main number to the first number on the analog rotary. Toggle one switch next to the CSU/DSU, and we've got phone service.

Wireless to the Warehouse

Our old building was about 15,000 square feet, the new building about 50,000 square feet.

Running cat5 out to the warehouse in the old building was no problem. The new building, however, was a different story. The distance for running cat5 exceeded recommended guidelines. Wireless didn't work well because of all of the metal racks and high-stacked inventory. So we designed a simple compromise. Cat5 from computer room to a WAP at the front of the warehouse, then WAP at the rear of the warehouse to a router, with no obstructions in between. Problem solved.

Network Certification

I've seen some estimates as high as 50% of all network failures are actually cable failures. In our case, since everything was brand new, it was essential we test our LAN right down to each and every cable. Somehow we were able to borrow a cable tester from a well known company that builds them, at no charge (they run several thousand to tens of thousands of dollars). Basically, you "buzz" out one cable at a time, the cable tester on one end, a termination device at the other end, and record the results. Out of several hundred separate cables that had been pulled through conduit, we found only a few that failed.

Chronic Phone Problems

Moving to a brand new building versus one that's been around awhile is the difference between night and day. Most of the problems are due a brand new, untested, infrastructure. And, most of the problems seem to be contained primarily to electrical and communication issues. We were one of several brand new buildings which had been built within the same period of time in the same new industrial park. Prior to development of this new park, the land was wild. One of the more annoying ramifications of relocating to a brand new industrial park was the constant interruption in services.

As new buildings were added to the "grid", various services would fail. Although our intention for the investment in a large UPS was for power failure caused by over demand, it ended up working out very well for these other events.

Because the land had never been previously developed, there were numerous issues with flood control, or lack thereof. I'll never understand why the Telco couldn't anticipate the "B" box at the bottom of the hill might just get flooded out from time to time. It couldn't have been situated in a better location for flooding had it actually been planned. And, that meant every time it rained, we lost T1. Again, the redundant analog lines meant for emergencies paid off. This situation became such a nuisance, I actually visited neighboring buildings and figured out who would go down and under what circumstances. This helped me ultimately determine the cause of various failures.

One of the more interesting notes about infrastructure Snafu's was that the telephone lines for about two dozen neighboring buildings, including T1, terminated in the phone room in our building! I figured it out after wondering why there were so many punch-down panels. I took a butt set and started connecting to each of the punch-down blocks, and low and behold, I could listen in to every conversation! Apparently, the Telco fouled up when the cable was originally laid as there were hundreds of twisted pairs terminated in our building. I can only imagine what the expense would have been to fix it. To this day, I don't know if they did.

As you may know, it can get somewhat challenging to get a Telco technician on-site even of you know the problem is on their side of your phone system. You're under constant threat that if the failure is on your side, you will be liable for any labor and material charges. Even then, you can spend a good chunk of time pleading your case.

I solved the problem by pulling an old DOS notebook computer out of the scrap room and building a cable (RS-232). The cable connected the serial port on the notebook to the NCIC board in the telephone room. Once Hyper-Terminal was launched, I could run all the diagnostics on the NCIC. This allowed me to prove my case over the phone with the Telco, and I never had a problem getting a technician on site in a timely manner.

Chapter 24 Children and the Internet

Although a bit out of the scope of this guide, I mentioned in the About This Guide I would share a few tips about children and their exposure to the Internet.

My daughters' introduction to the Internet didn't begin until after most of her friends had been allowed access. This served as a barometer for me simply because I never had to deal with this issue before. In this way, I let other parents decide the age of the child, appropriate content, functionality to be allowed, and how much supervision there should be. My approach was gradual. I began with teaching her the basics of the Browser. We discussed what information was appropriate for her to view, and what type of content that was definitely not appropriate. I tend to trust most folks until they give me a reason not to, so it wasn't too long before I let her have her own email account. She learned soon after (on her own) how to deploy Instant Messaging. As of this writing she will turn twelve soon, but I haven't yet allowed her to set up accounts on any of the social networking sites.

I played a prank on my daughter, perhaps objectionable to some, but it taught her an important lesson and it was hilarious anyway. I setup a fictitious email account, something like maryluvsdogs@mail.com and sent my daughter email pretending to be one of her friends. I purposely misspelled and abbreviated words as an eleven year old might, and to my surprise she was fooled. We emailed back and forth for about a week until suddenly on a Saturday afternoon she exclaimed loudly "Mom, this isn't Mary, are you doing this?". Now, mom doesn't know much about setting up email accounts, so it couldn't have been mom.

My daughter proceeded to spend the next several hours on the phone with her friend doing a "CSI" thing trying to figure out who the culprit was. She finally figured it out when she got to the last phony email stating that her dad is "a really cool guy". Needless to say, she is now wary of everything on the computer.

Here's another tip: I setup fictitious accounts on social networking sites so I can confirm privacy settings on my real account and potentially for use checking my daughter's account.

Chapter 25 Striking Out on Your Own

Ever thought about starting your own consulting business? All of us at one time or another wonder what it would be like to work for ourselves, collecting all of the accounts' receivables instead of getting only a paycheck and having to work for a boss.

The boss part is understandable, but take into consideration that as a Help Desk Tech, everyone is your boss. They include all of the in-house staff, customers, and corporate management. The only thing you gain being on your own is essentially eliminating the person that otherwise signs your paycheck, and maybe in-house staff. Remember that the customer is always right, and they're always the boss.

I have learned from my own experience having my own show one must consider the overhead involved with running your own business. Unless you are well capitalized, you will now be responsible for your own financial issues. From purchasing equipment and office supplies, to paying the phone bills, you will now be the boss that signs these checks in addition to your own. Depending on the circumstances, you may need to incorporate, LLC, or DBA. In any event you will likely need a TIN (Federal tax ID) just to open up a checking account, let alone for tax purposes. There may be legal issues, at least initially. For example, if you are selling software, you will want to obtain a "boiler plate" disclaimer to help protect yourself from any litigation. While you may be able to do most of this online, it may be worth a substantial invoice from an attorney just to make sure.

Do you have a business plan? Business plans include a detailed description of what your new organization will be engaging in now, and for the next five years.

If you're going for venture capital, or other form of capitalization, you will need to include income projections for at least the next five years. There are entire books dedicated entirely to formulating a business plan.

And the dreaded taxes. Again, depending on circumstances, you may be required to file, and pay, quarterly income statements with the State and Federal governments. Retaining every scrap of paper, including receipts, bills, invoices, purchase orders, and sales orders for the past seven years is recommended. Find out what you can write off, like depreciation of equipment, equipment purchases, and travel expenses.

Planning on working out of your home? At least at the time, I could have legally written off a room in my two bedroom cabin. But whatever you write off must be exclusively for the business. The room can't double as the game room, a bedroom, or any other room for personal use. In my case, this wasn't practical to begin with. Be wary of the tax man if you do decide to write off part of your home, because for all intents-and-purposes, the tax man's file on you will come up flashing on his computer screen come tax time.

Chapter 26 Quality Standards Policy

I'm probably going to upset some folks with this one as I know there are adamant proponents of QSP, but I'm entitled to my opinion. There really are companies which exist who pay tens of thousands of dollars each year for outside consulting firms to assist with establishing a Quality Standards Policy for every department in the organization. The ultimate goal of achieving a "successful" QSP is acquiring a "stamp of approval" from a well known organization for placement on marketing materials and web sites. The purpose of the great "stamp of approval", in theory, is to maintain the current client base while gaining new clients by presenting "certified" evidence of superior products and services above and beyond the competition.

The concept of developing a QSP is to document and maintain procedures with regards to virtually every aspect of daily operations. The theory is that by establishing procedures and policies which must be followed consistently be all employees at all times, will result in better quality products and services. The procedures and policies can be changed. However, due to the hierarchy of procedures and policies, changes must be accomplished by a system of approvals beginning at the ground level by supervisors, followed by department managers, and ultimately the Director of Operations and CEO. All policy and procedure changes must be documented on forms conforming to the QSP, and must also be signed off by the QSP Administrator. And, on perhaps a quarterly basis, the representative from the consulting firm, aka the Auditor, spends a couple of days reviewing changes to the QSP, policies, and procedures thus making sure everything "matches". I was always amazed at how consistently low the error rate was reported by the Auditor.

Could this have anything to do with the tens of thousands of dollars per year paid out to the Auditor?

QSP ultimately morphs into something called Quality System Standards (QSS), whereby the company receives the all-important "stamp of approval". This whole concept is a quagmire of paperwork, considerable lost time in employee productivity (each department must be audited internally prior to the quarterly visit by the consulting Auditor), and based on my experience QSS has never produced any discernable impact in terms of improving corporate revenue (other than the out-going tens of thousands I've already mentioned). Of course, there is never any mention about how one might measure such results. In addition to audits performed by the outside firm, internal audits must be performed by employees delegated that responsibility. Employees are also required to record any human errors, even their own. And guess what happens when employees learn they have to record and post their own errors? Even though employees are assured time and again this audit trail will have nothing to do with their evaluated job performance as an individual employee, they never buy it. I had one experience where an employee actually edited her department error log, deleting most of her own error entries. Essentially, this system is wide open for corruption because the bulk of the data accumulated is the responsibility of each employee. Even though the intent is clearly not to expose or punish human error, human nature says otherwise.

As the Assistant IT Manager at a small distribution company and engaged in light manufacturing, I also had to fill in as the QSP/QSS Administrator. In order to keep the "stamp of approval" current, the entire Quality System Policy infrastructure must be maintained (and paid for) basically forever, or until the economy tanks as it did beginning 2008.

While the intent of QSP/QSS is to allow the organization to evaluate itself by "drilling down" its internal data to expose weaknesses, subjecting employees to what amounts to continuous interrogation is simply not productive and does nothing to improve moral.

In summary, the concept of quality control doesn't have to be defined by an entity outside an organization. You can acquire and deploy identical guidelines without having to waste hundreds of people hours per year to do so. Besides, I thought this is why we have supervisors, supervisors have managers, and managers have senior executives.

Appendix A Writing this Book

I've actually self published another eBook for Kindle. The book is a camping guide targeted at novice campers who just want to spend time outdoors but don't really know how to get started. I had already composed most of this guide on Help Desk when I decided to switch back to completing the camping guide thinking it would be simpler to do and use it as a learning experience to finish the Help Desk Guide. Well, I was wrong. The camping guide is image rich, and was difficult to get it into an acceptable format. I had to pick up more than just basic HTML to finally get it to an acceptable level of quality, at least by my standards.

Thanks to my technical background, I was able to persevere, and frankly, I'm glad it's not a trivial task thus eliminating a substantial amount of competition. If you're considering self publishing, I encourage you to do so. However, beware the many books, free articles on the Internet, and so on that supposedly provide information on how to self-publish eBooks. None that I have found was actually able to take me from start to finish. The technology as of the time of this writing is too dynamic even for eBooks to keep up with. I think you'll find you will have to work a little harder and use your professional skills to overcome the obstacles.

Appendix B Sample Letters

This is a very basic welcome letter that I use when delivering software to a new client. Remember, the check has been deposited, so no need to sell the system all over again:

May 25, 2010

Donald Brown
President
Nuts and Bolts, Inc.
3442 Main Street
Tucson, AZ 85704

Dear Donald,

Welcome to the Acme Widgets family of users, and congratulations on your purchase of your Acme Widgets Platinum Package!

Please find enclosed CD's containing Acme Widgets, and your Acme Widgets Modules. Also included is a CD containing the Relational Database software, and the Acme Widgets User's Guide in PDF format.

Installing Acme Widgets, and the Relational Database application is quick and easy. Once you decide where you want Acme Widgets to reside on your network, installation takes less than 30 minutes. We will assist you with the initial setting up of your publication so you'll be able to start exploring Acme Widgets right away!

I will be in touch soon to arrange a time convenient for you to assist with the installation of your Acme Widgets Platinum Package. I would also be delighted to schedule some time, perhaps an hour or so, to give you an introductory tour of Acme Widgets to get you started.

I know you will be pleased with our timely response to all of your Acme Widgets support requirements.

Should you have any questions, please don't hesitate to drop an email or call.

Regards,

D. Russell Steffy
Software Support Specialist
1-800-555-1212
drsteffy@acmewidgets.com

Sample Update letter

Again, remember, the check has been deposited, so no need to sell the system all over again. The primary purpose of sending hard media updates periodically is to provide something the customer can physically handle:

May 25, 2010

Donald Brown
President
Nuts and Bolts, Inc.
3442 Main Street
Tucson, AZ 85704

Dear Donald,

Please find enclosed a CD containing the latest version of Acme Widgets 7.0, your version 7.0 Acme Widgets Modules, and a CD containing the Relational Database applications.

Please note that it may not be necessary to reinstall or change any Relational Database components for this update. The Relational Database software has been included as part of our procedure and is intended primarily for your files in the event it is required.

Please let me know when it might be convenient for me to connect via the Internet and assist with the installation of this upgrade.

Regards,
D. Russell Steffy
Software Support Specialist
1-800-555-1212
drsteffy@acmewidgets.com

Sample Upgrade letter

May 25, 2010

Donald Brown
President
Nuts and Bolts, Inc.
3442 Main Street
Tucson, AZ 85704

Dear Donald,

Please find enclosed a CD containing the latest version of
Acme Widgets 7.0, your version 7.0 Acme Widgets
Modules, and a CD containing the Relational Database
applications.

Please note that it may not be necessary to reinstall or
change any Relational Database components for this
update. The Relational Database software has been
included as part of our procedure and is intended primarily
for your files in the event it is required.

I will be delighted to assist you with the installation of your
new upgrade. Please let me know when we can schedule a
day and time convenient for you for this installation.

Sincerely,

D. Russell Steffy
Software Support Specialist
1-800-555-1212
drsteffy@acmewidgets.com

Appendix C Sample Resume

Due to formatting constraints, I am unable to format my sample resume to one page which is what I recommend;

D. Russell Steffy | Los Angles, CA 90290 | (818) 555-1212 |
drussel247@mail.com

Applications: Access, ACCPAC ProSeries, ACT!, Active Directory, Adobe, Excel, Exchange, FrontPage, Informix, InstallShield, Outlook, Symantec, Pervasive, Veritas, Word. ISO 9000.

Operating Systems: DOS, PRIMOS, TSO/ISPF, UNIX, Windows 95,98/NT/2K/XP, 2K/2003 Server, TCP/IP.

Programming Languages: 8088 Assembly, BASIC, FORTRAN, MS Developer Studio; Familiarity with FoxPro, VB and C/C++.

Hardware: 3Com NBX, CDC Cyber, Cray, General Automation, IBM 3090, Intel, Dec PDP/VAX, Prime, Varian.

Employment

8/05 – Present   **Media Management, Inc.** – Senior Software Support Technician

> **Environment:** Windows XP/Server2003, Access, Excel, Word, Pervasive, Veritas
> I accelerated the stabilization of our flagship product by overhauling customer support techniques, setting up test cases and stepping through source code locating problem areas prior to submission for correction, and effecting rigorous testing of software corrections. The result was a 20% decrease in call volume in my first year, followed by a similar drop in each of the subsequent years. I now enjoy helping increase our corporate revenue by focusing more attention on data conversions for new business, and billable custom projects for existing accounts.

4/00 – 8/05   **ACME Products, Inc.** – Assistant Manager of Information Technology

> **Environment**: Windows 95/NT/2K, 2K Server, TCP/IP, Exchange, Outlook, Access, ACT!, Excel, Word, FOXPRO
> I contributed to the design of the computer facilities, including location of power and network cable conduit, telephony (VoIP, and redundant analog as an

emergency backup system), fire suppression, HVAC, and security systems during the construction of our new building, while achieving 99.7% network uptime. I successfully lobbied against the purchase of a gas turbine backup electrical system in favor of American Power Conversion's Symmetra, saving the company over $200,000 in near term expenses.

3/94 - 4/00   **Finance Technologies, Inc.** – Manager, Product
Support

Environment: DOS, FORTRAN, MS Developer Studio, Visual C++, Windows 95/98
I successfully ported a DOS application containing over 200,000 lines of code to Windows 95 in less than two man-years. The port included replacing the original text driven interface with the latest Graphical User Interface written in C. The production code for the proprietary database engine and report generators remained virtually untouched resulting in an extremely stable initial Windows release, and allowing the company to maintain a competitive edge.

4/85 - 3/94   **Portfolio Systems, Inc.** – Manager, Product
Development
                Environment: 8088 Assembly, DOS, FORTRAN, Informix, OS2, Windows 3.x
In 1988, I correctly decided against porting existing applications to OS/2 as I did not consider this a practical platform for the foreseeable future. The following year, I correctly perceived another large competitor to Windows as playing a minor role for hosting commercial applications. As a result, I realized a savings of over $2,000,000 for SDK's, licensing, and overhead. This budget was instead earmarked for further development of existing Unix based applications which continue to be successful today.

Education:
Santa Monica College, 1978-1981. Coursework included studies in computer science and mathematics.
TriNet Networking and Training, Inc. 2003-2004, Microsoft Certified Systems Engineer

Publications:
"Feature Extraction From FLIR Imagery", SPIE's Annual
International Symposium,
Image Processing for Missile Guidance, SPIE, Vol.238, San Diego,
California, July 28 - August 1, 1980.
"Portfolio Systems User's Guide", Portfolio Systems Inc, 1986
"Fine-tuning Performance With Portfolio Management Software",
Research Magazine, Vol.17, No.10, San Francisco, California, October
1994.
"Finance Technologies User's Guide", Finance Technologies Inc,
1994

Other: U.S. Citizen; DoD Secret/ Top Secret (inactive); ISO 9000, lift
50lbs

Appendix D Sample Cover Letter

Dear Madam, Sir,

I am responding to your posting for a position as your Help Desk Technical Support Superstar. Please find my attached resume for your perusal. I am seeking a challenging position in Customer Service with emphasis on Information Technology.

I enjoy over twenty years of experience in the commercial software industry and in organizations funded by various branches of the United States Department of Defense. I have assumed roles as an applications programmer, network administrator, team leader of product development and product support. All of my positions have been with small to medium sized companies which has allowed me to gain exposure to all departments within the organization such as Sales, Marketing, Inventory and Warehousing, and Accounting. I have had the distinct opportunity to consult on all aspects of company operations for purposes of optimizing processes pertaining to a given department from an Information Technology point-of-view.

I am well versed in commercial software applications that support the financial services, circulation and fulfillment, and light manufacturing industries. Among my strengths are excellent organizational, time management, problem solving, and telephone skills. My ability to communicate technical issues to all levels of users is always appreciated. I possess a broad knowledge of applications and current technologies including many industry standard Windows-based applications. When necessary, I utilize the Knowledge Base and FAQ features of large product vendors on the Internet, in addition to using search engines, to assist with the problem solving process.

Other relevant experience includes documentation of software source codes, user's manuals, and ISO 9000 procedures and work instructions. I have a general knowledge of hardware at the component level.

I believe my experience over a broad base of industries, coupled with my skills in applications programming, network administration, and a focus on providing excellent client support makes me an excellent fit as your Help Desk Technical Support Superstar!

Thank you for your time, and I welcome the opportunity to further discuss how my skills may be of benefit to you and your organization.

Sincerely,

D. Russell Steffy
(818) 555-1212
Los Angles, CA
Druss247@mail.com

Appendix E Training Itinerary

This is a generic agenda that I have put together when called upon to provide training to new employees, entry to intermediate level staff, and tutoring jobs on the side. I hope you find it useful.

History of Computers, basic concepts of evolution
        Vacuum tubes, to transistors, to IC's, and miniaturization and thermal dynamics
        Peripherals including drum, disk, paper tape, tab cards, floppy disks

Navigating Windows

Files and Folders
        File Maintenance (copying, renaming files, folders, just like a filing cabinet). Organize locations for specific file types for purposes of backing up.
Peripherals (printers), Hard Drives (Physical, Logical), Memory, CPU
Backup and Restore
Control Panel; Add/Remove Programs

Networking

Operating Systems
        What is an Operating System?
        What is a network?
Windows
LAN
WAN

Microsoft Office

Word
Excel
Access
PowerPoint
Outlook, setting up Email, Using Task Manager

Utilities

Compressed Files
FTP (File Transfer Protocol)
PC to PC Connection Applications
Administrative tools, My computer, Manage
Hard Drive defragmentation
Delete temporary [internet] files
Adobe Reader, Acrobat
Managing Digital Pictures
Burning CD's, DVD's

Internet

Copy/Paste a link into the Browser
Cached Page
Using Search features in Knowledge Bases and FAQ's

Security

What are viruses?
What are spybots?
Anti-virus and Adware applications
Internet Explorer vs. Other Browsers

Appendix F Boiler Plate Support Agreement

SUPPORT AGREEMENT

Acme Manufacturing, Inc. (Hereafter referred to as "Customer")

Effective Date:_____
To:_____

Covered Software: ABC Widgets Software Accounting Package (SAP)

SAP Base System
Five Workstation Licenses
Zip Code Database
SAP Import Module

1. General Intent. ABC WIDGETS, INC.(Hereafter referred to as "COMPANY") will provide Customer with the software support services and products described herein.
2. Services Provided by COMPANY.
 A.Software Releases. Customer is entitled to updates developed for COMPANY software that are incorporated into software releases for the major version at the time of purchase. Updates may include new features, software corrections, and/or rule changes. When applicable, COMPANY will provide Customer with these updates with instructions describing update procedures. Updates are defined as version updates, for example, 6.1 or 6.2. COMPANY may charge additional fees for major Upgrade Versions of the system (Upgrades such as from Version 6 to Version 7).
 B.Software Information. Customer is entitled to a free subscription to the COMPANY newsletter and internet site with important information regarding use of the COMPANY software.

C.Reporting Software Requests. If a problem develops with standard COMPANY software products, or Customer wishes to suggest a software enhancement, Customer may submit a Software Request form to COMPANY. COMPANY will acknowledge receipt of the Software Request and notify Customer of its disposition. COMPANY reserves the right to determine, in its good faith discretion, what significant problems warrant correction or revisions to be included in future updates.

D.Telephone Support. COMPANY will provide telephone assistance to Customer in the use of covered COMPANY software products, in identifying problems, and providing possible workarounds. The hours of coverage for regular telephone response service are 8:30 a.m. to 5:30 p.m., Pacific Standard Time, Monday through Friday, excluding COMPANY holidays. North American customers may use COMPANY's toll free line. COMPANY will use good faith efforts to return calls as soon as possible, and to promptly respond to facsimile or e-mail requests. Priority will be given to customers based on severity of issue, for example, assistance with installation of COMPANY applications due to Customers' equipment failure.

E.Training and Custom Programming. COMPANY will provide training, on-site support, custom programming, or other services as requested by Customer subject to COMPANY'S standard rates and procedures.

3. Prerequisites and Limitations of Service.

A.Customer Contacts. COMPANY requests that Customer use a designated system manager and one alternate who have been trained in operation of the COMPANY software as contacts for COMPANY.

B.Supported Software Version. COMPANY will provide support only for the current version, and the one (1) version immediately preceding the current version, of COMPANY software products.

208

C.Non-Qualified Software. "Non-qualified software" is any software not supplied within a standard COMPANY software release, any software developed by a third party, or any software that has been modified by Customer or a third party. Free support for non-qualified software is not provided under this agreement. Customer is solely responsible for the compatibility of non-qualified software with covered software products.

D.Data Recovery. Data recovery and data input are not covered. Data integrity is Customer's responsibility and will not be assumed by COMPANY or any COMPANY employee, regardless of the cause of the data loss. Customer agrees to maintain backup procedures external to COMPANY software products to ensure a means of data recovery.

E.Force Majeure. COMPANY shall be under no obligation to furnish services or products under this Agreement should support be required because of (1) improper use or equipment problems; (2) natural disasters such as flood, fire or earthquake; (3) strikes, riots, acts of war, electrical disruptions, or nuclear disaster; (4) repairs, maintenance, modifications, or relocation and reinstallation made by other than COMPANY personnel or without COMPANY's supervision and approval; or (5) other causes beyond COMPANY's control.

F.Exclusions. COMPANY's support services do not include (1) operating supplies and consumables; (2) electrical work external to the software; (3) maintenance of accessories, attachments or products not specified herein; or (4) any other services not specifically described herein.

4. Software Use Limitations and Copyright Restrictions. COMPANY hereby grants Customer a non-exclusive, non-transferable, and non-assignable license to use any software enhancements, updates, modifications or manuals supplied by COMPANY under this Agreement.

Such use is limited to use of the software only on the specific central processing unit or computer designated in Customer's Software License Agreement. Customer shall not (1) alter, decompile, disassemble, or reverse-engineer the software, (2) use the software on upgraded or additional central processing units, (3) copy the software except for reasonable backup purposes, and (4) shall not disclose, disseminate or transfer the software to any third party. Customer specifically acknowledges and agrees that all software provided herein is the proprietary and trade secret property of COMPANY, and COMPANY has all rights and title to such software including the right to protect by copyright or to reproduce, publish, sell, license and distribute the same. All rights to the software not specifically granted herein are reserved to COMPANY.

5. Term and Renewal.
 A. This Agreement shall commence on the specified Effective Date and end upon termination by either party as provided in this paragraph 6.
 B. Either party may terminate this Agreement effective as of the end of this six month term or future term by giving written notice of termination to the other party not more than ninety days (90) not less than thirty days (30) prior to the end of the term. Additionally, COMPANY may terminate this agreement if Customer is in breach of this agreement, or any other agreement entered into with COMPANY, and Customer has not cured such breach within thirty (30) days of delivery of written notice from COMPANY.

6. Warranty for Support Services
 (A) COMPANY agrees it will provide software support services and products to Customer on a "good faith" basis.

(B) THE WARRANTY SPECIFIED IN THIS AGREEMENT IS IN LIEU OF ALL OTHER WARRANTIES, EXPRESSED OR IMPLIED, INCLUDING BUT NOT LIMITED TO ANY IMPLIED WARRANTY OF MERCHANTABILITY OR FITNESS FOR A PARTICULAR PURPOSE.

7. Charges. Unless otherwise stated in writing by COMPANY, Customer shall pay all invoices issued by COMPANY in full, without offset, within thirty (30) days from date of invoice. Customer agrees to pay for COMPANY's reasonable out of pocket expenses including without limitation charges for postage, overnight delivery, replacement media and additional manuals. Licensee shall be liable for payment of all sales, use or other taxes, however designated or levied, based on the services and products provided under this Agreement, exclusive of taxes based on the income of COMPANY or on the ownership rights held by COMPANY concerning its software. The charges due under this Agreement are payable in advance. Future annual support renewal will be at the rate of (TBD) annually for the covered software.

8. Limitation of Liability. COMPANY IS NOT LIABLE FOR SPECIAL, INCIDENTAL, CONSEQUENTIAL, INDIRECT OR OTHER SIMILAR DAMAGES, EVEN IF IT HAS BEEN ADVISED OF THE POSSIBILITY OF SUCH DAMAGES. IN NO EVENT SHALL COMPANY BE LIABLE FOR DAMAGES OR COSTS INCURRED AS A RESULT OF LOSS OF TIME, LOSS OF DATA, LOSS OF PROFITS OR REVENUE, OR LOSS OF USE OF THE SOFTWARE. COMPANY'S LIABILITY FOR DAMAGES TO CUSTOMER FOR ANY CAUSE WHATSOEVER, AND REGARDLESS OF THE FORM OF ACTION, WHETHER IN CONTRACT OR IN TORT, INCLUDING NEGLIGENCE, SHALL NOT EXCEED THE AGGREGATE OF THE CHARGES PAID BY CUSTOMER TO COMPANY UNDER THIS AGREEMENT ALL OTHER AGREEMENTS. THE FOREGOING LIMITATIONS ON LIABILITY AND DAMAGES APPLY REGARDLESS OF ANY FORM OF THE CLAIM BY CUSTOMER, INCLUDING A CLAIM THAT ANY WARRANTY GRANTED IN THIS AGREEMENT HAS FAILED OF ITS ESSENTIAL PURPOSE.

9. Miscellaneous.

A. Assignment. Customer shall not assign this Agreement without the express written consent of COMPANY, which consent shall not be unreasonably withheld. Any attempt to assign any rights, duties or obligations under this Agreement, without such consent, shall be null and void.

B. Forum. The parties agree and consent to jurisdiction and venue in Clark County, State of Nevada for any suit brought to interpret or enforce this Agreement, or to confirm an arbitration award.

C. Interpretation. Section headings are for convenience only and are not a part of this Agreement. This Agreement is to be interpreted as if it were jointly prepared by all the parties hereto. This Agreement is to be construed in accordance with the laws of the State of Nevada.

D. Entire Agreement. This Agreement contains the entire agreement and understanding concerning the subject matter hereof between the parties, and supersedes and replaces all prior negotiations, proposed agreements and agreements, written or oral. Each of the parties hereto acknowledges that no other party hereto nor any agent or attorney of any such party has made any promise, express or implied, not contained in this Agreement to induce them to execute this Agreement. Each of the parties further acknowledges that they are not executing this instrument in reliance on any promise, representation or warranty not contained in this document.

E. Authority. Each party executing this Agreement represents and warrants that they have the absolute authority and power to do so and each other party may rely upon such representation and warranty in executing this Agreement.

F. Successors. The terms of this Agreement shall be binding upon and inure to the benefit of the respective successors and assigns of the parties hereto.

  G. Severability. If any provision or term of this Agreement is determined by a court of competent jurisdiction to be illegal or unenforceable for any reason, such determination shall not affect the validity of the remaining provisions or terms.

  H. Waiver. No waiver by any party of any default shall be deemed a waiver of any subsequent default.

  I. Amendments. This Agreement may not be amended or modified except by a writing signed by the parties affected thereby.

10. During the Term of this Agreement [and for six (6) months hereafter], neither party shall directly or indirectly solicit or recruit any employee or consultant who has been introduced to the other through performance of COMPANY Services hereunder, either for itself or for any other company or individual, without the prior written consent of the other; provided, however, that nothing stated herein shall be construed to prevent either party from (A) soliciting any such employee or consultant of the other Party who has been terminated by such other Party and/or (B) hiring any such employee or consultant of the other Party resulting from:(i) advertising of open positions, participation in job fairs or the like, or other form of soliciting candidates for employment which are general in nature and not directed specifically or soley at a given employee of the other party; (ii) solicited inquires about employment opportunities or possibilities from agents acting for unidentified principals or (iii) unsolicited inquiries about employment opportunities from such employee or consultant.

IN WITNESS WHEREOF, the parties hereto have caused this Agreement to be executed as of the dates indicated:

```
Acme Manufacturing, Inc.
Signature: _____
Name:
Title:
Date:    _____


ABC Widgets, Inc.
12345 Apple Street
Las Vegas, NV 80025 U.S.A.
Signature: _____
Name:
Title:
Date:    _____
```

Appendix G Job Descriptions, What They Really Mean?

Have you ever given a second thought as to what those job descriptions actually mean? I didn't until well into my career. I like to peruse the employment ads regularly just to keep an eye on my industry, and its one more barometer on which to gauge the economy. One ad I found, for presumably a very small company, touted one of their perks: "Holidays? We work'em all!". What a great way to attract real talent.

So, I have put together a list of job descriptions followed by definitions the way I interpret them, maybe a little more realistically. Perhaps this can save you from wasting a day of filling out applications for a position you may not land, and be glad you didn't:

Description: Fast paced, dynamic environment.
Definition: Perpetual SNAFU.

Description: We are looking for people who fit but who do not conform.
Definition: What the heck does that mean?

Description: If you want to be part of a fast-paced team…
Definition: How many in the team to support how many users?

Description: A+, MCSE, CCNA, .Net. MSSQL, Linux.
Definition: All that for $15.00 an hour?

Description: Multitask efficiently, work under pressure.
Definition: You're going to be a one person IT department.

Description: Problem solve accurately and efficiently.
Definition: How does one problem solve inaccurately?

Description: We work hard, lean and smart…
Definition: You'll be cleaning the bathrooms in your "spare" time.

Description: Challenging position…
Definition: The only guy that knew anything left, you'll be on your own.

Description: We are looking for candidates interested in expanding their career horizon.
Definition: Your only training will be provided by your users.

Description: This is a unique position, starting as a part-time position, but with huge growth potential.
Definition: No budget for a full time position. They are in financial recovery.

Description: We are looking for an energetic, enthusiastic, quick learner…
Definition: Forty and over need not apply.

Description: Future plans on advancement are imminent if we find the right person.
Definition: "Bottom Feeder".

About the Author

Mr. Steffy has over 25 years of providing non-technical and technical support to all levels of users. His experience includes providing hands-on assistance to in-house staff, over-the-phone support to product end-users, and technical training in a corporate classroom environment.

Mr. Steffy began his career in 1972 as an RJE (Remote Job Entry) Operator. During the 1970's, he taught himself Basic, Fortran, and 8088 Assembly, and gained experience on more than two dozen operating system and hardware environments.

The 1980's introduced the first affordable PC's running DOS along with a need for professional Help Desk Technicians for commercial industry, and the challenges of interacting with a diverse cross-section of general population. Windows-based operating systems introduced and accepted in the mid 1990's offered a much needed unwritten industry standard by which software applications, technical documentation, and technical support would evolve towards greater efficiency and less-complex learning curve for users.

Alas, the twenty-first century, finding itself in a PC-saturated world driving the forces that be, to create new versions of operating systems requiring the purchase of new hardware, in turn causing software developers to spend resources beyond comprehension so products will continue to run in the new environments. And, of course, one step before the end of this food chain, the Help Desk Tech must continue to stay savvy for the benefit of the end user.

This guide can be construed as Mr. Steffys' professional autobiography. Indeed, it is based on first hand experiences over a significant span of time within the evolution of digital computers, operating systems, software applications, and users. The purpose of this guide is to share his experiences that go well beyond the class room by offering real world solutions for everyday Help Desk issues.

Acknowledgments

To my wife Gloria, who when asked which way to turn to get to her friend's wedding: "Honey, do we turn right or left here?" Response: "Yes!".

And to my daughter Laura, for whom I set up her very own account on the family computer and then asked me repeatedly what her password was. I kept telling her the password is "SECRET". I could never figure out why she couldn't memorize such an easy password.

To my good friend Steve, a very analytical, no nonsense guy, posed perhaps the most challenging philosophical question I have ever encountered: "In two sentences or less, give me a definition of 'Common Sense'".

And to Frank, you can't get any closer than a brother. Rest in Peace Bro.

Index